MARANATHA

C. S. Lovett

MAN

C. S. LOVETT: MARANATHA MAN

AN AUTOBIOGRAPHY

author of

Dealing With The Devil
Soul-Winning Made Easy
Jesus Wants You Well!
"Help Lord—The Devil Wants Me Fat!"

cover photos by Linda Lovett

published by
PERSONAL CHRISTIANITY
Baldwin Park, California 91706

ACKNOWLEDGMENTS

My special thanks to my dear wife, Marjorie, for
the hours she spent in helping me gather the
material for this book. To her goes credit for all
the pictures you'll see, for she sifted through
piles of photos to select the ones we used.
Also much credit goes to Robert Paul Lamb
for his part in organizing and laying out the
story. His gifted writing skills contributed great-
ly to the flow of the narrative.

PRINTED IN THE UNITED STATES OF AMERICA

Contents

What mother, holding her child, doesn't wonder what he will become. Here is Agnes Lovett with her firstborn, C. S. Lovett, at five months.

CHAPTER ONE

Almost A Murderer!

Inside of me was a wild restless urge. There was a terrible void in my soul. It drove me to awful things. Before I could understand my own actions I had yanked a .38 from my belt and was aiming it at a 14 year old boy.

The other kids stared in shocked approval as I held the loaded gun to the head of a rival gang leader...and squeezed the trigger.

"Click."

The hammer fell on a dud. The gun didn't fire. Why? God didn't want C. S. Lovett to go to jail as a murderer. But I didn't know that then. I was only fourteen myself.

How could I do such a thing? Looking back, I see how the stage was set for me to become a criminal the day I was born.

* *

Being raised in a rural area is no guarantee a youngster won't get into trouble. I had the privilege of being born in one of the nicest little towns in California. Some one hundred-eighty miles north of Los Angeles and midway between Fresno and Bakersfield is Tulare. Situated in the heart of the fertile San Joaquin Valley, this community of 5,000 people was an assortment of general stores, gas pumps and railroad tracks. I was born October 26, 1917, not far from where the Southern Pacific and Santa Fe railroads cross each other.

I was named Cummings Samuel Lovett after mother's dad, Cummings Samuel Nicewonger. Grandpa owned considerable property around Tulare, where he and my father, Clyde A. Lovett, were in business together operating an Overland car dealership.

Dad was a crafty salesman with few business scruples. He wasn't above selling the same car to two or three different people—collecting the money from the buyers, but never delivering the promised automobile.

The Nicewongers were originally from Holland, migrating to California by way of Pennsylvania. Grandma was born in Inverness, Scotland. Dad's side of the family were Scots too, coming to New England from Glasgow. I understand a lot of Lovetts are still scattered from Massachusetts to Maine.

My parents' marriage was shaky from the start. They

8

had met in church, but dad told me years later he had gone there for the sole purpose of finding a girl. He wasn't the church-going type but he knew that was the place to find a "decent" girl. His choice was pretty, golden-haired Agnes Nicewonger, my mother.

My grandparents had given their only daughter the best of everything—clothes, schooling and social graces. In marrying Clyde A. Lovett, who obviously had none of these things, they felt their daughter had married beneath herself. They predicted the marriage would fail.

Maybe they even took some satisfaction when the fragile marital foundation dissolved completely after my brother, Fraser, was born thirteen months following me. My dad left Tulare and, at their urging, mother moved us in with our grandparents.

The next few years passed routinely for the five of us. The large, two-story Nicewonger house was surrounded by grassy yard shaded by large oak trees. Since the yard was unfenced, mother often tied her two boys to an oak tree to keep us from wandering away.

One day when I was about five years old, a shiny black car drove up. When a swarthy-looking man called out *"Hi kids,"* Fraser and I innocently strayed in his direction. Curiosity drew us to him. *"How'd you like some toys?"* he asked, without getting out of the car.

We were too little to suspect anything when the back door opened and he urged us to get in. Fraser and I stepped onto the running board and seated ourselves behind the smiling stranger. *"We'll just have to go and get them,"* the man said driving off down the road in a cloud of dust.

Instead of going for toys, as he promised, the man drove several hundred miles north to San Francisco. Once there, he farmed us out to various "foster" families whom he paid to care for us from week to week. We didn't realize it, but we'd been—KIDNAPPED! We thought all those strange people we lived with were relatives. He instructed us to call them "uncle" and "aunt."

During the next year, we were shuffled from one house to another. No one actually mistreated us, although one family locked us out of their house. We spent several cold nights among the sand dunes of San Francisco Bay living off wild strawberries.

Christmas was approaching. At the time, Fraser and I were staying with a poor family. The father worked at a cannery. It was a cold Sunday afternoon. We were stringing popcorn with the family to make ornaments for the tree, when a knock at the door interrupted our fun.

Before we knew it, our mother, accompanied by several uniformed policemen, walked into the room. Fraser and I ran to meet her. Tears gathered in mother's eyes and ran down her face as she swept us into her arms and hugged us. I thought she'd never stop kissing us.

Mother had frantically searched for us throughout the entire year we'd been missing. She never gave up. Finally the police got a lead, tracing us to San Francisco, and then to the right house. The kidnapper turned out to be a former business associate of Grandpa Nicewonger.

10

There had been a dispute over a land transaction and the kidnapping was an act of vengeance. Inasmuch as we were unharmed, the abductor escaped prosecution.

Fraser and I had no sooner returned to Tulare than mother moved south to Los Angeles. An only child, she had been sent to teacher's college. Los Angeles was the closest place she could find work in her chosen profession. We stayed behind living with our elderly grandparents. This was a decision that would haunt mother for years to come.

Here are Fraser and I close to age 9 and 10. A terrific bond had developed between us.

Grandpa was a stocky man with a wide mustache and wavy white hair. He had a gruff manner and that's the way he treated most people, except me. As his namesake, I qualified for a special place in his heart. The two of us would spend hours together. I loved those times when we'd sit on the front porch swing and he'd tell me stories or we'd walk the few blocks into town for his daily trek after cigars.

Already in his late fifties, Grandpa's health was fading. He had a bad heart and it put him to bed for long periods of time. With his being sick so much of the time, Grandma had her hands full taking care of him. As a result, she couldn't watch over her grandsons to give them the supervision they needed. That gave Fraser and me too much time on our own. With the freedom to do whatever we wanted, it was inevitable we'd get into trouble.

It all started simply enough.

I was riding on the handlebars of George Hick's bicycle one day when he suggested we stop off at Triplett's general store for a candy bar. As kids will do in a small town, we sauntered through the place nibbling on our candy bars, looking over the assorted merchandise. George casually picked up several packs of BB's.

"Put'em in your pocket," he whispered, thrusting the BB's at me.

I hesitated, but the older boy was insistent. Feeling pressured, I reached for the BB's and shoved them into my pocket. I nervously finished my candy bar and walked outside. I wasn't ready for what came next.

"Now, Sam, you're going to give me some money," George threatened as he pedalled back down the street. *"If you don't, I'm gonna take you to the police station and tell them you stole those BB's! Boy, will you get it!"*

"But......" I started to protest.

"I mean it," he said forcefully, jabbing a fist into my ribs.

In panic I submitted to his demand. I went home, took my piggy bank and opened it with a knife. George was waiting on the front porch and I handed over the money. *"See, you're not so dumb,"* he said walking off with a triumphant air about him.

It was a beginning for me. A beginning that would ultimately lead me into crime on my own...and set in motion by this one bullying experience with George Heck. At 13, you're not ready to cope with blackmail.

But George wasn't finished with me. He continued to extort money from me for months afterwards. The threat of exposure was an efficient weapon in his hands. I endured it until the moment arrived when I had enough.

I was coming home from school one day when George approached me again. I knew what he had in mind. Well, this time I had a weapon ready—my roller skates. As the older boy started his familiar brow-beating, something inside me erupted and I angrily swung the skates at his head.

He tumbled to the ground in a heap, blood gushing from a wide cut in his forehead. Kids who had been watching us, expecting to see me pushed around, scat-

13

tered in every direction. A bloody, dazed George Hick looked up at me as I dangled the heavy metal skates over his head. *"Don't you ever try to pull that on me again,"* I said through clenched teeth. *"I might kill you next time."*

George picked himself up and stumbled home, never to bother me again. Word quickly spread around Tulare that "Sam" Lovett was nobody to fool with. With a reputation like that, it was easy to organize and lead my own gang.

With Grandpa becoming more and more confined to bed with his heart condition, Fraser and I became bolder in our activities. Tulare was surrounded by vineyards and large open fields of alfalfa. Small game abounded and we became experts at hunting with .22 rifles. But more often we used our marksmanship to shoot out electric lights in rural farm houses. A dangerous thing, to be sure. But we were thriving on danger by now.

At night we got a big kick out of burglarizing the stores in town. Since we were not big in size, it was easy to pry open a window and wriggle inside. The cash box was our first target. But if money wasn't handy, we'd take any merchandise we thought useful.

Sometimes we planned gang raids just for kicks. Once we raided backyards and stole all the clothes pins in town. Stores ran out of pins causing a strange panic. The police were mystified. On another occasion we broke into a plumbing yard and made off with all the bathroom commodes. Later that same night we carefully draped them over the fireplugs along main street. A few months later we topped that by setting fire to the local ice house.

In spite of our undisciplined lives, Grandma insisted on some things—like going to Sunday school. We had a free hand during the week. But Sunday morning it was off to the Congregational church. Sometimes, in outlandish defiance, I carried a pistol in my pocket. Imagine sitting listening to a Bible lesson, with a gun pressing against your thigh.

It was in Sunday school that I first heard about Jesus and what He had done for mankind. The teacher, Mister Ledbetter, said Jesus was the Son of God. I had no trouble with that. It seemed like a historical fact—like Columbus discovering America. There was no reason to doubt it.

My activities with the gang grew more sinister and vicious. The day I came close to being a murderer, several of us had seized a rival gang leader and had him tied in a chair. We were trying to make him talk. Someone had squealed to the police about the stealing in Tulare. I thought it was this kid.

"Talk!" I demanded.

When he refused, a satanic mixture of pride and stupidity swept over me and out came the gun. I meant to use it. My finger actually pulled the trigger. But God, praise His name, overruled my wickedness, keeping me from becoming a 14-year-old murderer. He saw the vacuum in my soul, driving me like a restless wind. The ache in my spirit was responsible for the bizarre behavior.

15

Unknown to anyone but me, I longed for a father. I wanted a dad so badly. It seemed like other kids were always talking about their fathers. It tormented me to hear their stories. I was actually jealous when different ones complained of being spanked by their dads. I wanted a dad who'd whip me. I wanted a dad who'd take me camping and be a pal to me. I needed someone to tell me how to grow up.

I knew I had a real father somewhere. Fraser and I would talk about him late at night in the room we shared. We wondered where he was and what he looked like. But for years to come, he was to remain invisible, a mystery. Someone we were never supposed to see.

Our grandparents were always telling us what a worthless bum he was. *"No good, that's what he was,"* Grandma would say. Somehow I didn't want to believe that. My dad couldn't be like that. I guess it was because I wanted a father so badly.

Occasionally there were signs of a real dad. Once, two brand new Iver Johnson bicycles were delivered to our home. They were gifts from our unseen sire. Our grandparents were so upset they wouldn't allow us to ride those bikes for almost a year—simply because they were a gift from *"that awful man."*

Our father had also opened an account for us at McAllister's, an ice cream parlor. We were supposed to have free use of the account. But the same thing happened, Grandpa and Grandma forbade us to use it.

I was mystified by my grandparents' actions.

A growing frustration gnawed at my insides. My

16

troubles seemed to be pushing me on a collision course. In school I was often in hot water with the teachers for shooting off my mouth. Outside I was a campus brawler, in one fight after another. My gang activities intensified. Store burglaries and stealing became commonplace.

How I loved my grandfather, shown here with **Grandma Nicewonger**, who was the only mother I knew until I was 15 years old.

Then a rather minor incident was used of **God to bring** my criminal career to an end.

One night I had sneaked into a guy's backyard and stole his bicycle. Back home, I disassembled the bike,

17

replacing the parts with others I'd stolen previously. Then I took it down to a bike shop to be sold. That's where I slipped up.

Unfortunately for me, the bicycle had an unusual pair of handlebars. A visitor in the shop thought he recognized them. At least it was enough to make him suspicious. Shortly the police were knocking on our door asking to look around.

The officers were polite, actually apologetic in talking to Grandpa. He was highly respected in town, and they dared not tread on that. They checked around the yard and then disappeared into the garage. Within a few minutes they were back at the door.

"We've found some pieces of the missing bicycle in your garage," one of the men announced tersely. *"It looks like your boys might be involved."*

Grandpa called me. I walked nervously with him to the garage, along with the two policemen. *"A fellow by the name of Glenn Griggs gave us those handlebars,"* I volunteered, trying to lie out of the situation.

The four of us were discussing this when Fraser walked up. *"I was just telling these policemen how we got these handlebars from Glenn Griggs,"* rushing to get the words out before Fraser could say anything. It was obvious I had given myself away. The cops were quick to sense it. Grandpa did too.

I walked away, heading for the back porch. I could hear Grandpa and Fraser talking to the officers. I was caught—for the first time. Would the police find out about my other crimes? Had my criminal escapades

18

finally caught up with me? I knew I was in trouble now. Big trouble.

Tears stung my eyes. I could still hear Fraser trying to alibi. The situation was clearly hopeless. I might even be headed for jail or reform school. And then it happened to me...as it has to others...I found myself on my knees talking to that God I'd heard about in Sunday school.

"God, if you'll get me out of this, I'll never steal again," I pleaded, tears running down my cheeks. *"I promise. I won't ever steal again."* I meant it, too.

Time dragged as I waited for something to happen. I didn't know how God would answer or if He would. I knew nothing of His ways. Finally I gathered my courage and walked back out to the garage. Grandpa, Fraser and the two policemen looked up. *"I took the bicycle,"* I confessed sadly. *"Fraser had nothing to do with it."*

A pained look came across Grandpa's face. He cleared his throat.

The police weren't anxious to press the case. *"If you'll see that the bike is fixed up, Mr. Nicewonger, and returned, that's all that will be said."* They agreed between themselves, *"We're ready to forget it."*

Grandpa's status in town had been a lifesaver. He paid to have the bicycle renewed and the episode ended. But the relationship between him and me was wrecked— never to be the same again. He valued the worth of a man's word and I had been caught lying. Grandpa was crushed.

As for me, I knew my days of stealing and running

with gangs were over. I had made a promise to God; a promise I knew had to be kept. He had delivered me and there was something about Him that made me fear to break my promise.

No, I didn't know who God was, or for that matter where He was. But from that one incident, I knew HE WAS, and that He was powerful enough to get me out of trouble. That alone gave me cause to mend my ways.

CHAPTER TWO

"Lovett, What Are You Good For?"

After years of living alone in Los Angeles, mother remarried while Fraser and I were still living in Tulare with our grandparents. She and her new husband, Henry Pugh, drove up for a visit shortly afterwards.

Fraser and I were in the backyard talking about the recent addition to our family. *"What are we gonna call him?"* he asked, referring to our new stepfather.

"I sure wouldn't mind calling him dad," I ventured, undoubtedly speaking from the deep longing in my heart for a real father.

"Yeah, I wouldn't mind either," Fraser replied.

21

"But how would we do it?" I questioned. "We just can't walk up and start calling him dad."

He nodded his head in agreement, "Well, whatever we do you do it first, you're older."

"Maybe I can think of some way," I said, swallowing hard.

We walked over to Henry's new car. It was a Whippet. I ran my hand over the shiny finish beneath the dust which had settled on it. Fraser and I looked all over for a starter button. There didn't seem to be one. Ah...now I had a question I could ask Mr. Pugh.

I worked up my courage and shouted, "Hey, dad!"

Nothing happened. So I shouted again, not as shaky this time..."Hey, dad!"

Moments later Henry appeared in the doorway. "What is it?" he asked, a knowing smile creasing his face.

"Where's the starter on your car?"

"It's in the horn button," he answered. "You have to pull up on it to make it work."

It was sort of reassuring to have a dad. Henry seemed to warm to the idea. Even though he had four daughters by a former marriage, he treated Fraser and me as though we were his own. During the summers, when school was out, he and mother would come to Tulare to see us.

There was little contact with mother otherwise. It

22

gave me a rootless feeling. Sometimes at night I'd lie silently in my bed listening to the sound of a train whistle blowing in the distance. I wondered if I caught one of those trains would it take me to the thing my heart was seeking. It seemed like I didn't have a mother at all. Even though there was a big age difference, Grandma seemed more like my mother than anybody else.

Time was running out though. Change was in the wind.

Word ultimately got back to mother about our problems in Tulare and in 1932, Fraser and I moved south to live with her and Henry. I was 15 years old.

Probably by depression standards, the folks were doing well. Just to have two people working at good jobs was a big thing in those days. Armies of people had no job or were on WPA. With mother teaching school and my stepdad working for Texaco, they bought a large, comfortable two-story duplex in West Los Angeles. That made room for us.

Both of our grandparents died within months of each other shortly after Fraser and I moved. It seemed to me the whole world ought to know a good man died with Grandpa's passing. His big funeral somehow acknowledged that fact. Everybody in Tulare turned out. But funerals have a way of making you think of life and death.

Such thoughts were fresh in my mind months later when I traveled with my stepfather. As an engineer, part of his job was to inspect bulk gas storage tanks. This trip included a loop of the entire state of Arizona.

Towns like Bisbee, Lowell, Globe and Buckeye as well as Tombstone and Flagstaff.

On one occasion, we were staying in a cabin in a small mining town and I had some hours of free time. Behind the cabin a mountain rose hundreds of feet high. I decided to climb it. Something in me always wanted to see what was on top of mountains or on the other side.

It was hot. A bright sun hung overhead. No clouds. Enormous blue sky. I climbed steadily up the barren, iron-colored rocks. On the summit, I found the entrance to an abandoned mine. Heavy timbers jutted from the opening. A rusty iron bucket on wheels sat on tracks running from the mine. An ore car lay on its side.

A solitary bird soared overhead riding the air currents with its outstretched wings. I looked back at the town. Some of the houses looked no larger than matchboxes in the distance. The sky seemed endless. I leaned against the ore car, my thoughts drifting aimlessly. Then—suddenly—thunderous questions came down on me from nowhere...

"Who am I? Why am I here?"

An awesome awareness that there was more to life than I could understand swept over me. Why, there had to be more to me personally than I could fathom. *"I must have some reason for existing,"* I thought. It was a haunting feeling to think that something as big as life included me. But how? I had never been struck by such engulfing feelings before. *"What did it mean?"*

The thin line separating life and death became more real to me when I had a close brush with death at the age of seventeen. My stepfather was on vacation from his job with Texaco and we were visiting in Tulare headed for the mountains. Without any warning, I became nauseated and started vomiting.

Mother recognized I was very sick and in great pain. The doctor was called and he promised to come right over. But somehow he delayed and I grew worse.

Finally I struggled to the phone myself and called. *"You gotta come, doctor,"* I begged, *"I'm dying."* By the time the doctor arrived, the pain was so intense I was twisting and writhing on the floor like a snake.

"We can't wait for an ambulance," the doctor said after feeling my abdomen. *"He has a swollen appendix. We've got to get him to the hospital now."*

With the doctor's help, Dad Pugh and Fraser managed to get me into the car and to the hospital. But not in time. The appendix ruptured before the physician could operate. Deadly poison spread through my body.

"I really don't think we can save him," an anxious medic told mother, *"but we'll try."*

Darkness enveloped me for days. When I awoke, tubes were running from my body. I was a drainage case. My stepfather was seated in a nearby chair. *"How do you feel, Sam?"* he asked, standing up and walking over to the bed.

"I don't know," I answered faintly.

25

"The doctor said we almost lost you."

"Really?" I mumbled.

"It looked bad for awhile," he said.

Days later I learned that my stepfather had never left my bedside. He'd been there praying for me constantly. I knew him to be a dedicated Christian, one who read his Bible and listened to gospel radio programs like Charles E. Fuller of the Old Fashioned Revival Hour. His sacrifice in keeping vigil at my bedside touched me.

But why was my life spared? That was a puzzle. I had lingered at death's door, apparently. Why didn't I die? I wasn't a good guy like Henry Pugh. I was selfish, calloused, totally indifferent to others and their feelings. I thought only of Sam Lovett.

But dad Pugh was different. He thought about others. *"Why couldn't I be like him?"* I asked myself. *"Well maybe one of these days I'll find out what it is that makes him so different."*

One of those days never came though. I healed quickly from my appendectomy and soon the noble thoughts of being like my stepfather were shoved to the back of my mind. Although I had just barely graduated from high school, I made plans to enter Santa Monica Junior College.

I really don't know why I enrolled. I wasn't interested in getting a degree. I studied very little. If a project had to be turned in, I'd put it off until the very last moment. I was more interested in girls than anything else. That was a subject I pursued with seriousness.

Fraser worked part-time for a boat builder. His ability to create things was incredible. There was magic in his hands. Our mutual joy was a blue and white sailboat Fraser had built. I loved to sail and spent as many days on the water as I could. The college was but a few blocks from the harbor where we kept the boat. I often cut classes to take girls sailing. You can guess what that did to my school work. It took me almost four years to graduate from a two year junior college.

Henry Pugh, my stepfather, was a godly man who exerted a powerful influence on mother and her two boys. He was the only dad I knew for 10 years.

During the summer months Fraser and I worked with our stepfather constructing gasoline stations for Texaco. We still lived at home with mother supplying all of our monetary needs during the school year. It was as though she were trying to make amends for the years we lived apart from her. We got a generous weekly allowance. She even went so far as to purchase a car for us.

The depression was ending with President Roosevelt in office but jobs were still hard to get. I had submitted applications to businesses all over the West Los Angeles area. One day I walked into a nearby Safeway grocery market and applied.

"Do you have any experience?" asked the employment officer.

"Sure," I answered confidently, *"I've been in Safeway for three years."* He thought I was talking about job experience but I was referring to the fact that I had shopped in Safeway for mother that long. I was pleased with the little deception.

On the basis of that one statement, Safeway called me in several weeks and I reported to one of their stores. I was as green as the lettuce in the produce section. I didn't know the first thing about working in a grocery store.

One of the assistants saw me wandering about. *"Grab an apron,"* he said commandingly, *"the load's on the floor."*

"Right," I responded, though I didn't have the slight-

est notion of what he meant. *"Load? Floor? What aprons?"* I silently asked myself. It was all Greek to me.

I wandered down another aisle. A different employee cornered me. *"Man, if you don't get to work, you won't be here long. Why don't you work over there? Those boxes have already been opened."* Obediently I walked to the spot where he had pointed and began putting cans on the shelf.

The assistant reappeared in a few minutes. *"Oh, there you are,"* he said. *"I wondered where you went. What are you doing here?"*

"The other guy said the load was in," I replied, *"and he thought I ought to get on it."*

"Yeah," he smiled approvingly, *"I'm glad to see you're working on it."*

So far so good. I now knew what the load was—a shipment of goods to be placed on the shelves. As I stacked row after row, I listened to the others talking, trying to glean what might be expected of me. Another assistant walked past. *"They need you up front,"* he ordered, motioning with his hand. Oh oh, I knew even less about handling produce.

I wandered to the front of the store where a clerk was trimming cauliflower. I picked up a knife and started doing the same thing. Being inexperienced, there was little cauliflower left when I got through with it.

"Hey, go easy on those things," he said laughing, *"leave enough to sell."*

"Sure, sure," I agreed. *"I guess my mind was on something else."*

In a few days I learned the ropes. I had actually gotten a job without a single day's experience. I had pulled it off on the basis of sheer daring.

I had bluffed my way through a job situation with a smiling, self-confident attitude, but inside it was a different story. There were many questions I couldn't answer. Questions about life. Questions about death. Questions about eternity.

My parents coaxed Fraser and me into attending the Wilshire Presbyterian Church. We went along just to please them. But one day I was asked to pray before a Sunday school class. I almost choked getting some words out. It was enough to make me quit—so I did. The embarrassment was pure torture.

Months later, I was home alone on a Sunday morning. Fraser had gone down to the boat. The folks were at lunch. I was in the shower getting ready for a date. As the warm water relaxed me, my mind drifted to the life ahead of me. I found myself in the same mood as that day on the mountain. Once again—a thunderous question came down upon me...

"Lovett, what good are you?"

I'm sure it didn't come from my own thoughts. Rather it seemed to come from outside me. I wouldn't ask myself that question. It was too penetrating. It probed where I didn't like to look.

The hot water splashed against my head as I leaned

closer to the nozzle. The question wouldn't go away. It bounced in my thoughts for a long time. I didn't like the weight of it. I lied frequently. I used people. I was always scheming and manipulating others. Not to mention the girls. Boy did I ever like girls. All of my worldly activities were flashing before my mind.

The painful question persisted, *"What good are you to anybody?"*

I thought long and hard. I wasn't any good to my mother. I was living at home just using her. Whatever I got from mother, I took selfishly and coolly. Even Fraser—I constantly used him. That was my trouble. I used everybody. There were no exceptions. I had five girls on the string each thinking she was the "only one."

For the first time in my life I took a good look at myself and saw what I really was. Worthless. Nothing. A bum. No good to anyone. At first I was tempted to think...*"Awh, it can't be that bad. There's some good in everyone."* I didn't want to face the truth. But there was no way around it. *"Lovett, you really are worthless,"* I finally admitted to myself. *"You're no good to anyone."*

The hot water was beginning to cool. I turned it off and stood in front of the electric wall heater drying myself slowly. *"What am I going to do with my life,"* I wondered. *"I can't keep going on like this. My life has to count for something."*

The question continually stirred within me. It generated a combination of feelings I would learn to live with for years to come.

CHAPTER THREE

Up In The Wild Blue Yonder

"R-R-R-R-R-I-N-N-G-G." "R-R-R-R-R-I-N-N-G-G."

It was the telephone and I hurried to answer. *"Probably one of the girls with big plans for the weekend,"* I said to myself, hopefully. I spent most of my time either making plans with girls or attempting to carry them out. Girls were my passion now.

"Sam?" a man's voice was at the other end.

"Yes, who's this?"

"This is your father speaking."

MY FATHER!

My heart skipped a beat. I was speechless. The voice at the other end of the line was saying he was my father. All of my life I'd heard what a bum he was supposed to be. *"No good,"* my grandmother had said continually. They frequently reminded me my dad was out with another woman the night Fraser was born.

Now at age 21, I was hearing the voice of my real father whom I hadn't seen since infancy. Inside I had often wondered about this man who'd left such a vacuum in my soul. The things my grandparents did—refusing us the bicycles, preventing us from going to the malt shop and always running him down—served only to intensify my curiosity about him. By the time his telephone call came, a buffalo stampede couldn't have kept me from seeing him.

Finally I blurted out, *"Where are you?"*

"At the gas station down at the corner."

"I'll be right there," I volunteered quickly.

I knew mother would never approve of my meeting my dad, but that made no difference. I deeply resented being kept from him all these years. It seemed so unfair.

Minutes later I was looking into Clyde A. Lovett's blue eyes. I shook his hand, carefully searching to see if I could recognize some physical resemblance. Fraser and I had often speculated as to which of us looked like him. Now I knew—it was I. And what a resemblance. I was a dead ringer for him—light sandy hair, medium build, about six feet tall. It was uncanny.

"How are you?" he said smiling. *"Are you getting*

along okay?" He seemed to be as nervous as I and just as full of questions.

"Fine, fine," I answered.

"That's good, that's good." The words weren't coming easily yet.

"What about yourself," I inquired. *"Where do you live? What do you do for a living? Do you have a family?"*

"I live in the south end of Los Angeles," he said, wiping a sprig of wind-blown hair from his eyes, *"and I'm in the building business. To tell the truth, I've made several fortunes and lost them. But now I've found a way to make money building motels and I'm climbing back up again."*

"Hey, that sounds great," I said enthusiastically.

"I came to Los Angeles a couple years ago, absolutely broke," he continued. *"I even had to sleep in my car while looking for work. Then I found a man who needed a roofing job. I traded the job for a vacant lot the man had. I built a house on the lot and that's how I got started again. I've got a motel that's doing well and things are rolling now."*

"Wow, that's terrific!" I responded.

Dad was a sparkling conversationalist and I was intrigued by his personality. He had a strong determined way about him in spite of his past business reversals. I admired his attitude. He seemed unconquerable.

He invited Fraser and me to his house for a visit.

34

Thereafter my brother and I saw my dad and his wife regularly. He eventually offered to teach us the building business and we saw a way to do something with our lives. The idea of learning the construction business intrigued us.

We figured what dad was doing was "really living." We wanted to be part of it. In spite of all we'd heard about him, we were now ready to disbelieve it all. We were like pieces of metal drawn to a powerful magnet. The attraction was tremendous.

C. A. Lovett, my natural father, whom I met for the first time when I was 21 years old. You can see why I was struck by the resemblance.

When she wasn't teaching school during the summer months, mother traveled with our stepfather. This time when they returned from an extended trip, we had already moved out of the house. We went back one day to give her the startling news—we had met our real dad.

Poor mother, she was devastated. Her face turned ashen. Her eyes filled with tears.

"I know it's an awful shock to you," I admitted, *"but Fraser and I want to go work with our real father."*

Years before, dad had told her he would come back one day and take her boys away from her—and sure enough it was happening right before her eyes. That made the situation even worse.

"If that's what you want to do," she said through trembling lips, *"I can't stop you. Go ahead."*

Mother would have supported us financially for the rest of our lives if we had stayed. But now she was crushed. Things would hardly be the same between us after that. An invisible barrier was now separating us. In some ways she still didn't seem like our mother. We'd gone too many years without her. So it wasn't hard for Fraser and me to do what we wanted. We were so caught up in the power of our new excitement, her feelings were of little importance to us.

But if our relationship with mother wasn't normal, our involvement with our real dad was just as strange. I wasn't personally drawn to him as a father. He was more like a man I respected and admired, rather than someone I could love. I was more awed by the thrill of discovering my real father than by the man himself.

Once we left home, however, we had an immediate struggle on our hands. Dad wasn't the patsy mother had been. He was interested in helping us, but he wasn't about to spoil us any further. He wouldn't hand out money as mother had. He provided a small apartment for us to live in for about three weeks. The arrangement was temporary. He expected us to get out and make our own way.

"That's part of being men," he exhorted us. *"Nobody gets ahead in this life without hard work."*

I still had my job with Safeway and Fraser, with his excellent mechanical skills, joined Menasco Engineering. Dad quickly recognized how spoiled we were. So while teaching us the construction business, he threw in a few lessons on life as well. Particularly on how to handle money.

Fraser and I were so thrilled with meeting our natural father, that we left our mother and joined dad in the building business.

War clouds were gathering in Europe during the late 1930's. Hitler was beginning to gobble up the small countries. America's war industry was cranking up as planes and other materials were needed in Europe and Asia.

After starting with Safeway at $10.65 a week, my pay gradually increased to $18.00 a week. I ultimately reached the place where I was drawing the princely sum of $22.00 a week. Fraser and I restricted ourselves to two meals a day and one on Sunday. We tried to live as frugally as possible. We knew it would bring big dividends one day.

After leaving dad's apartment, we moved into our own on the corner of Pico Boulevard and Hauser. We were seeing first hand we could make it on our own. We saved our money and learned rapidly as dad taught us the "ins-and-outs" of the building trade.

It was a successful combination. Fraser was a master craftsman, talented at drawing plans. I had a knack for spotting sites and making deals. We were a swell team. We also did much of the construction work ourselves, organizing crews for the concrete and carpentry work. The rest was done by sub-contractors.

Dad's strategy was to build a motel, run it for a short time, and sell it on the basis of its income rather than the cost of construction. The profits were huge that way. He built about 28 of them around town and we gained a lot of experience working with him.

While at first he constructed motels only, he later shifted to large apartment buildings. As Fraser and I watched dad put together a new fortune, we decided to

38

do the same. With our earnings we bought a piece of property on Centinela Avenue near the Douglas Aircraft plant.

Dad had taught us how to approach the lenders for building loans and we were able to borrow enough to construct eight double apartments. Being near the aircraft plant, which was getting busier by the day, our units rented immediately and we had income property. It was the first of many for the Lovett Brothers.

The war raging in Europe and in the Orient was getting closer to America's shores. During 1941 the government began offering pilot training. It was called Civilian Pilot Training (CPT). If a person had two years of college and was 21 years old, the government would give him flight training free of charge.

Our training began at Mines Field (later to become the sprawling Los Angeles International Airport). The field was only a short distance from our new apartments. A collection of small flying schools and repair shops ringed the airport with its single paved runway. Our training was relegated to grass and dirt landing strips. The field was laced with rabbit trails disappearing into the cabbage and alfalfa crops stretching beyond the airport.

I was fascinated with flying. Yet, I didn't take to it as readily as I thought I would. For years I had read magazines on flying like "War Birds" or "Flying Aces." I just loved those stories. I thought a person could learn to fly simply by reading them.

It all seemed simple enough. I'd read how a pilot would make a left turn by giving it left stick and left rudder. Everybody knew you pulled back on the stick to go up and pushed forward to go down. *"Should be a simple thing to do,"* I thought to myself.

Yet when I climbed into place for the first time, I discovered there had to be a perfect wedding of hands and feet to make the airplane fly. In time, I was able to consumate that marriage.

At last the time arrived for me to solo. Cliff Bantel, a short stocky fellow, had been my instructor. *"Okay, Lovett,"* he said, crawling out of the small Taylorcraft. *"You take it."*

"All right," I responded confidently, but my heart was pounding through my shirt.

I pushed the throttle all the way forward and the plane headed down the grassy strip, slowly gathering speed. I guess I hadn't checked the runway carefully. Before I knew it, a farmer on a tractor was pulling a cultivator across the airstrip directly in front of me. What a spot for a fledgling birdman! I couldn't stop. And planes don't back up. Even though there really wasn't enough speed yet for the plane to fly, I yanked back on the stick at the last minute and pointed its nose into the sky.

"CH-CH-CH-CH-CH-CH-CH!" The tiny craft hung on its prop—the engine racing wildly. "CH-CH-CH-CH-CH-CH!" It paused momentarily, then staggered, almost stalling completely. I thought I was a goner.

Somehow the struggling little monoplane skimmed

over the top of the tractor by inches. I could see the farmer's eyes wide with fear as I went over him close enough to shake his hands. Now that plane should have stalled and crashed, but it didn't. It managed to stay in the air long enough to pick up speed and become airborne. Then I climbed for a little altitude so I could circle the field and land. My heart was somewhere around my shoetops as I struggled out of the plane.

"What kind of a solo flight was that?" gasped my instructor. *"I wasn't sure I was going to see you again."*

I looked at Cliff whose face was still deathly white. *"For a minute there, I didn't think so either,"* I agreed shaking my head in wonder. *"That plane should have crashed but it didn't. How come I'm still here?"*

The incident was to remain vivid in my mind for months. Throughout 1941 Fraser and I continued our flight training at Mines Field. We were logging a few hours every week. In the meantime, I had quit my job at Safeway for a better paying one at Doak Aircraft where I was making radio masts for AT-6 military training planes.

One Sunday afternoon I came home from work and was unlocking our apartment door, when a voice called out. *"Hey! Did you hear!"* It was the guy upstairs shouting. *"They bombed Pearl Harbor!"*

"Pearl Harbor," I yelled back. *"Who did? What are you talking about?"*

"The Japanese," he answered excitedly. I thought he was going to fall over the balcony railing. *"Hundreds*

41

killed and wounded. They've sunk our fleet! It's all on the radio."

"Are you kiddin' me?" I thought he was putting me on.

"No, it's true. We could be at war by tomorrow. Roosevelt is scheduled to speak to the nation. All the newscasters say he's going to ask for a declaration of war."

"Oh man, that'll shake things up," I said, thinking how such a mind-boggling event would affect my future.

Roosevelt went before Congress and asked for a declaration of war and got it. America was instantly plunged into the conflict ravaging Europe and South East Asia. New rulings were soon in effect. All civilian flying within two hundred miles of the Pacific Coast was suspended. That meant our flying days at Mines Field were over.

The owners of the flight school decided to relocate in Baker, California. Located midway between Barstow and Las Vegas, Baker was nothing more than a highway junction with two gas stations. It was smack in the middle of the southern desert. The flying field consisted of a leveled off plot of ground, four miles from the intersection. It boasted two rickety sheds that were pressed into service as a repair shop and office. The place was so primitive it didn't even have a wind sock.

Fraser and I weren't concerned about any lack of comforts in Baker. We had something more urgent on our minds. The draft had been instituted with the declaration of war and we were vulnerable. However, if a person was engaged in pilot training, he could be deferred.

There was a shortage of pilots. Since we were aiming for pilot ratings, the draft board deferred us. Thus we quit our jobs. Home for us would be a small house trailer for myself, Fraser and two flying buddies.

We had already learned the basics of flying—weather, navigation and emergency situations. Now we moved to a secondary level—acrobatics.

Even though I loved the thrill of flying, I often felt the plane was flying me. I wasn't the master I longed to be. Somehow I held back from making it do what I wanted. I knew that to enjoy flying at its best, the wings of that plane had to become an extension of the pilot. Those wings had to become my wings. In the desert that happened.

Flying shifted from a discipline to outright FUN! In the process, I became a full-fledged daredevil!

One of my favorite stunts was to drop down behind a fast-moving train, skim up over the caboose and then run the plane's wheels atop the freight cars. It was fun to see the consternation on the face of the railroad man in the caboose as he watched—his eyes the size of dollars.

Another bit of excitement was to scoot along a highway about 70 miles an hour and play "chicken" with approaching cars. A tiny movement of the stick and I'd zoom over their heads. But more often than not, they'd leave the road. There was no limit to our thrill-seeking. We would play "follow the leader," and sometimes that led to weaving in and out of the huge cables bringing power to the L.A. area from Hoover Dam. At other times, in formation with other planes, we'd swoop over flocks of nesting ducks. What a sensation—birds whizzing through the struts. Dangerous too.

My brother and I weren't sure what we were going to do when our training ended. You had to have one hundred sixty hours of flight time to receive a commercial license. The very day I reached that total, two big, shiny military aircraft circled the field and headed in for a landing on the desert strip at Baker.

"What in the world are they doing coming in here," I wondered aloud as I watched the heavy ships descend on our field.

Two beribboned colonels climbed out. The bright sunlight made their insignias dance on their flight jackets. The officers were a flying review board, scouring the country for pilots with commercial licenses. The Army Air Corps needed flying instructors badly.

"How'd you like to fly that big AT-6?" one of the colonels asked me.

"Man, would I!" I beamed, drooling over the sleek, 650-horsepower aluminum giant.

The plane was a low-wing, two seater. Compared to the type I'd been flying, the cockpit seemed like a living room. The aircraft had retractable landing gear, the kind where the wheels tuck up underneath when you're airborne. Its top speed was somewhere around 170 mph. My little trainer would barely do 80.

I strapped myself in the front seat while the colonel got in the back. We took off and I followed his instructions, putting the ship through a series of maneuvers calculated to show how well I could handle it.

"That's very good," the colonel announced when we

44

got back to the field. *"How'd you like a job?"*

"Sure," I responded quickly, not quite aware of what he meant. But I was ready for anything. Even though I didn't know what was ahead of me, flying that powerful AT-6 had whetted my appetite. The colonel produced a contract which I promptly signed.

Fraser and I never thought about doing anything without each other. It'd been that way since we were little. But I wasn't sure how he'd react to this, though he had successfully completed a check ride himself. *"I've decided to go for this instructor's program,"* I explained as I got him outside the shed.

"What do you think? You want to sign up too?"

"It's kinda fast," he replied, stroking his chin, *"but let's do it anyway."*

"That's great!" I exclaimed. *"The Lovett Brothers stay together!"*

Our decision meant reporting to Mather Field in Sacramento on September 10, 1942. It also meant Marjorie Seyring and I could get married.

We had met some eighteen months before at the Safeway store in Beverly Hills. I was working in the produce section between the squash and the potatoes, when I looked up one day into the sparkling blue eyes of a tall, slender, dark-haired beauty.

"Wow!" my heart skipped a beat. *"That's my kind of girl!"*

45

You can see why my heart skipped a beat when I first laid eyes on Margie.

Margie's mother was a regular customer, who somehow became impressed with my politeness. On an impulse she introduced me to her daughter, as they stood in line at the checkout counter. It wasn't long before I was invited to their home for dinner.

Her dad worked as a salesman, an outgoing fellow with a warm sense of humor. Her mother was a great cook and made me feel at home right away. Once I saw what Margie, an only child, was like in the home, I knew she was the one for me. In fact, I was so smitten with her I proposed on our very first date.

We had gone for a long drive, traveling up the coast and tracing our way back through the hills. We spent the whole afternoon together. Night came and we returned to the city for a candlelight dinner at a swanky, red-carpeted restaurant. Even though it was our first real date, the restaurant's atmosphere, plus Margie's close presence, propelled me into expressing my feelings.

"This may startle you," I said reaching for the right words. *"In fact, it may even shock you."*

"Oh," she replied softly.

"You're exactly what I want in a wife," I announced with a smile, *"and I want you to marry me."*

"You do," she said returning the smile.

"Yes, I really do."

Margie didn't say yes, nor did she say no. Her attitude was more that marriage might be a possibility. Since she was not yet 17 and I was only 23, I was willing to wait. It seemed so right, being together. I knew she was the one for me.

Six months later, it was definite. *"When I knew it was right,"* she said later, *"my heart fell ker-plunk."*

Margie operated our apartment business while Fraser and I were in the desert. Each weekend I drove the long distance between Baker and Los Angeles. I could hardly stand to be away from her. The decision to accept the instructor's job with the Air Corps, meant we could get married. Our future was now settled with respect to the war.

47

. . . and we were married September 4, 1942.

Fraser and I closed up shop in Baker and returned to Los Angeles. I'll never forget how excited I was driving to Margie's house in Beverly Hills. *"When can we get married?"* Those were the first words I shouted from the bottom of the stairs.

"I'm ready, I'm ready," she flashed back, running down the steps into my waiting arms.

She was full of questions. I hurriedly told her about the training program for flight instructors, and how Fraser and I had signed up for the duration of the war. There wasn't much time to get everything done before reporting to Sacramento. In the rush we forgot all about a wedding photographer.

Fortunately Margie knew the pastor of the United Presbyterian Church in Beverly Hills. We were married there on September 4, 1942. Our honeymoon was necessarily brief, so we spent it at the Biltmore Hotel in Los Angeles. Any place would have been fine. We were so much in love.

Margie went to work fixing up the house trailer we had brought in from the desert, a sixteen-foot Highway Pullman. She added cute little curtains, giving it a cheery woman's touch. Then we loaded the trailer, and with Fraser headed for Sacramento and a new beginning with the Army Air Corps.

Johnny Young, one of the pilots from our desert training at Baker, came to Mather Field too. We often took our planes out together and were forever dogfighting. Our favorite stunt was to start out at five thousand feet, losing altitude as we tried to get on each other's tail, pretending all the while to shoot one another down. Many other pilots enjoyed this combat tactic too.

One day, Johnny and I were flying low-wing Ryan PT-22s. We had worked our way down to about a hundred feet above the ground. It was time to break off and climb back up. But at the moment I was in a steep bank directly behind Johnny, trying to close in for a final burst of my imaginary machine guns. Suddenly I hit his prop wash. The turbulence flipped my aircraft on its back. I was upside down.

There was no way to roll out. I didn't have enough speed. I was almost stalled as it was. The aircraft nosed down. In my heart I knew this was it—I was going in. I needed more speed. So I pushed the stick forward— toward the ground. I had to get out of that dangerous propwash...and I needed speed. The plan was to wait until the very last minute and then pull back on the stick. But in a hundred feet? Impossible! I yanked the controls hard into my stomach—but nothing happened! That was it. There was no more room left. I was going in.

Then—mysteriously, miraculously—the plane some-how righted itself, climbing away from the earth.

Numb with shock at still being alive, I flew the plane back to Mather Field, landed and climbed out as fast as I could. My senses were in a daze. Johnny was right behind me.

My rubbery legs took me to a box not far from the runway. I sat there, my face buried in my hands. As Johnny came over to where I was sitting, I raised my

50

head and looked up at him. *"Johnny, did you see what happened?"*

His eyes were wide with unbelief. *"Yes, I saw it, but I'm not sure what I saw."* He was shaking his head, dumbfounded. *"There is no way in the world a plane can pull out of a dive with that little room. It's just not possible. Yet I saw it happen. I'd say it was supernatural."*

"Supernatural?" That brought up some feelings. *"You really mean it?"*

"I don't know what I mean," he said almost apologetically, *"but it was as if some giant hand took hold of your plane and made it climb abruptly instead of crashing into the ground. Some force just seemed to take over. I know it sounds crazy, but that's the way it looked to me."*

I nodded my head. *"Maybe you're right,"* I was yielding to the idea. *"There doesn't seem to be any other explanation."* Perhaps some higher power *was* involved. In fact, it had to be a power *higher* than the laws of aerodynamics.

"Well," suggested Johnny, *"whatever it was, to me it was a miracle."*

"I'm inclined to agree, Johnny, but maybe it would be better if we didn't say anything to anyone about this. People will think we're crazy."

Secretly my mind was prepared to consider the supernatural.

Months earlier, several of us pilots had been sleeping out under the stars in the desert around Baker. Everybody was speculating aloud as to what was behind the stars. Finally we agreed that Somebody or Something had to create them. They just didn't create themselves. From my Sunday school training, I had no trouble acknowledging that Someone to be God.

Then, more recently, I had toured the grounds of Forest Lawn Cemetary with a group of friends. Along one of the paths I had come face-to-face with an open Bible in marble on a white pedestal. Written across the gleaming white marble in bold letters were the words, *"Lo, I am with you always."* My eyes were riveted to those words. Somehow I sensed they pertained to me, yet there was nothing I could put my finger on. It took a shout from the group to break the spell and get me away from that Bible.

As I sat listening to Johnny's words about the miracle that had happened, these two seemingly unrelated experiences flooded back into my thoughts. *"Is God interested in me personally? Was the giant hand that saved me from death—His?"*

I had no ready answers to such thoughts. But somehow I felt the day might come when I would.

CHAPTER FOUR

Questions With No Answers

Throughout the remainder of 1942 and into early 1943, I trained at Mather Field. Then in February, I was assigned as a flight instructor to La Junta, an Army training base in southeastern Colorado located right on the Arkansas River.

My commission as a Second Lieutenant came through a month after my transfer. A strong feeling of self-consciousness flooded me as I pinned the gold lieutenant's bars on my blouse. The uniform even felt heavier when I put it on.

A few minutes later, Margie and I left for the base theater. As fate would have it, we passed an old, grizzled Army veteran. He sensed I was newly commissioned.

My graduating class at Mather Field, taken in front of an AT-6. Fraser and I are the two guys in the back row at the right (see arrows).

"There's a new one, there's a new one," he muttered loud enough for me to hear as we moved past him to the box office. My face flushed beet red. Margie beamed proudly.

Margie and I were proud of those lieutenant's bars.

The Air Corps had a policy of keeping brothers together so Fraser was also transferred to La Junta as a flight instructor. He was commissioned on the same date.

Weather was a real problem when we first arrived in Colorado. I was a California boy with a California wife accustomed to bright sunlight and balmy days. Neither of us was prepared for the frigid Colorado winter that descended upon us.

Our accomodations provided little relief from the elements. Fraser stayed in the officer's quarters, but since I was married, I rented a Howard trailer, a mobile home constructed with virtually no insulation. At night, we turned up the heat, piled on the covers...and still froze!

Many mornings snow drifts were piled against the door requiring much pushing and tugging just to get out of the trailer. Then I went through the usual routine of locating my car—most of the time a hump in the snow, penetrated by a radio antenna indicating where the car had been parked last.

In the end, we decided we couldn't survive another day in the trailer and moved to a motel in town.

La Junta was my initial assignment as a twin engine flight instructor. It was expected of an instructor that he would fly "by the book," but those daredevil instincts were still with me. I loved the sensation of trees, fences and landscape whizzing past as I flew a few feet off the ground.

It was fun working with the cadets, instructing them on the ground before we took to the air (top). My brother was in one plane and I in the other, as we passed over movie actor Edward Arnold and his party at La Junta, Colorado (bottom).

Southeastern Colorado's terrain is highlighted by swift-flowing rivers, waterfalls and deep gorges. It provided a fabulous setting for my daredevil stunts.

I thrilled to skimming along the surface of the ground at high speeds and coming to the edge of a canyon. As the ground vanished from under me, the sensation was incredible. Then I'd plunge straight down into the canyon, pulling out of the dive within a few feet of the water. With all that speed I'd fly vertically up the sheer walls of the canyon to emerge upside down. I felt just like an eagle showing off for her young.

I was out with one of my students, Sonny Hall, one day and we came upon a farm with a large corral filled with sheep. I pointed to the farm below us, *"I'm going to drop in on those sheep. Watch what they do."* Sonny looked at me mystified.

Banking the twin engine aircraft sharply, I dropped down low so that I would come suddenly upon the sheep from behind the barn. Skimming along the ground, we came up behind the flock. The sheep were so panic stricken they rushed together leaping high in the air. It appeared like a fountain of sheep shooting up and spilling over.

As I cleared the corral and banked to pass between the farm house and the barn, I was suddenly confronted with a row of tall trees.

Oh oh, I hadn't planned on that. With nowhere near enough room to clear those trees, I yanked back on the wheel, standing the plane on its tail.

"W-H-U-M-P! R-R-R-I-I-I-P-P-P!"

Tree tops reached up and shredded the fabric skin covering of the airplane's fuselage. The props were bent. The wings tattered underneath, barely giving enough lift to keep us in the air. The twin engines rocked dangerously in their cradles. I had to throttle back or they'd pull out of their mounts.

Wind screamed through the holes in the fuselage with a deafening whine as the plane shuddered and staggered long. Somehow I managed to get it level, but we were sputtering along only a few hundred feet high. The craft vibrated wildly as if connected to a jackhammer.

Sonny and I began "praying" simultaneously. *"Lord, don't let us crash. Please get us back to the base."* It must have pleased God to honor that "prayer," because it wasn't long before the runway was in sight. We both breathed a sigh of relief as the wheels touched down and the plane came to a stop.

I spent a silent moment in the cockpit, marvelling that my life had been spared once more. There it was again. The probing questions returned: *"Why me? Who am I to be singled out for such protection?"* But I shrugged off the spiritual perplexity with a sigh. I guess I wasn't ready for the answer—yet.

"You forget all about this," I ordered my wide-eyed student who still in a state of shock. *"I'm not going to fill out an accident form or make any kind of a report. We'll just see what happens."*

As we walked from the flight line, I heard the crew chief's bewildered voice. *"What in the world happened to my airplane?"* he exclaimed. I kept on walking, not daring even to turn around. I hoped for anonymity from the incident.

The next day a notice appeared on the instructor's bulletin board. "All accidents must be reported," the terse statement read. "Failure to do so is a court martial offense."

"Court martial offense," I gasped. *"Whew! I wonder if they have me in mind?"* For the next day or so I approached my mail box timidly. I was half-expecting a summons to the commander's office. Surely the crew chief had seen me. I know he saw the airplane. I never thought I'd get away with it.

Fortunately, at that very time, the twin-engine school was being shut down and transfers were taking place. I received word that I was to go to Yuma, Arizona. If that had not occurred, I don't know what might have come of the matter.

Like many other air base cities in the country, abruptly inundated with military personnel, Yuma was facing a housing shortage. Yet, Margie and I were able to find quarters with Ethel and Gene Moss in Somerton, a small community south of Yuma not far from the base.

The Mosses were lovely people; quiet, friendly, with a son in the service. They had just finished building a tiny cottage in their backyard. It was for servicemen. The rent was fifteen dollars a month. We cooked on a two-burner hot plate the whole time we lived there. It was Spartan, but Margie and I were happy together.

60

The tiny cottage in which we lived while stationed at Yuma Air Force Base. The existence was Spartan indeed, but it seemed like a palace to two young people in love.

With my transfer to Yuma, Fraser transferred also. The bond with him continued. We were still doing things together. In fact, we had purchased twin Cadillacs. The last Cadillac before the war was the 1941 model. They were selling brand new for eight hundred dollars.

Since gasoline was rationed, people frequently got rid of their big cars, because it took rationed gas to run them. We had connections for gas stamps, so we purchased two 1940 Cadillacs for a mere four hundred dollars each.

Even though my brother and I had our hands full as flight instructors, we never forgot the construction business, nor the practical lessons our dad had taught us. *"Learn to save your money and your money will take care of you,"* he often advised.

He taught us that money was not something you spent on yourself simply because you had it. It was a tool to be used. Therefore it was natural for us to invest our money in real estate.

At the time, we were making good money—about six hundred dollars a month with flight pay and various allowances as officers. I had managed to save about ten thousand dollars. Fraser had set aside five thousand.

Our classes consisted of six or seven cadets, and between each new class of students, the instructors were given a brief leave. On those leaves, we were allowed to take an airplane and fly anywhere in the United States. We took advantage of those leaves to buzz back to Los Angeles and invest our money in real estate.

New building was restricted because of the war effort. Construction of movie theaters, motels, hotels or cocktail bars was not allowed. As a result, the prices on commercial properties were severely depressed. A piece of property, zoned for business and worth perhaps fifty thousand dollars before the war, was now selling for only a few thousand dollars.

Fraser and I started buying up such commercial property making the lowest down payment possible and signing up for small monthly payments. We'd return to Yuma for our next class, finish that, and return to Los Angeles to buy more property.

For several months we continued pyramiding our real estate. We figured if we survived the war and price controls went off the commercial sites—the land values would skyrocket. If the prices didn't go up, we'd still have the locations to build on.

Survival was a key word inasmuch as flying was a hazardous business. Any flight could be your last. Once when I was "stunting" some thirty miles from the base in a Curtis AT-9 (fondly called a "lead duck" because of its slowness), I lost one of the plane's engines. Oil must have gotten into the combustion chambers. The engine sputtered a few times and then quit altogether. I made a feverish attempt to get it going again—to no avail.

I immediately headed back toward the base limping along on one engine. I say limping, because it barely flew with both of its engines. The plane dropped lower and lower to the ground. I wasn't sure we could make it. But just when I thought we might have to ditch in a rugged gulley, the runway suddenly appeared ahead and I came skimming over the fence. That was close. That "Mighty Hand" was still protecting me.

A number of pilots were killed around Yuma. Tiny asphalt triangles situated in the desert were used as auxiliary flying strips to relieve congestion at the main airbase. A pilot would fly out to one of these satellite fields and use his radio to control traffic in and out of that airstrip.

Many times that lone pilot would return to base late at night. Nighttime on the desert can really be dark. With no lights for reference, pilots sometimes lost their horizon and crashed.

Crashes weren't restricted to nighttime, either. Once I was with a squadron of planes on a low-level, cross-country run about three hundred feet off the ground. As I watched with horror, one of the planes in front of me made an abrupt dive and went straight in. Nobody was ever sure what happened. It could have been mechanical failure, or the pilot may have done it intentionally.

I'm not sure, but it was probably plane crashes that eventually drove me to church. The Mosses were regular churchgoers, always talking to Margie about our attending. One day she asked me if I would like to go with our kind hosts, and I agreed.

It was a small Methodist church in a white frame building, such as you see in the average rural community. That Sunday the church was having communion. The pastor, a middle-aged man, was explaining Jesus' death on the cross. It seemed like his firm, resonant voice was aimed directly at me.

Deep inside I knew—as never before—there was a connection between C. S. Lovett and that Man on the cross. Tears ringed my eyes and ran down my face onto my neatly pressed uniform. People around me shifted uncomfortably in their pews.

Before I knew it, my cup overflowed. I wept uncontrollably. My clothes became damp with my tears, but somehow I didn't care. Something inside me was crying to get out. I buried my head in my hands and sobbed.

The service ended. People slipped by quietly, staring at the emotional officer out of the corner of their eyes.

I felt a hand on my shoulder. I looked up into the condescending face of the pastor.

"Everything's going to be okay," he said patting me on the back. *"All you need to do is go home and get a little rest. You'll feel better afterwards."*

I didn't reply. I was trying to fathom my feelings. I couldn't understand why I'd react that way. Yet I couldn't shake the idea there was some connection between that Man on the cross and me. I wasn't aware of it, but my soul was begging for an introduction to Jesus. That's what was behind my tearful outburst.

Margie clutched my hand tightly as we walked from the church. She was as surprised as anyone at my tearful display. *"That was awful,"* I said, after we got home. *"I don't ever want to go through that again. It's too embarrassing."*

She sensed my inner distress and agreed, reluctantly I think. Unknown to me, Margie had been thinking about God. In fact she had been praying at night, without knowing whether anybody was hearing her childlike utterances.

I just wanted to put the ordeal behind me.

A few months later we were transferred to Pecos, Texas, near the western corner of the state. The stay in Pecos turned out memorable—highlighted by the birth of our daughter, Linda Marjorie, one snowy morning in January of 1944.

Linda was one hour old when she posed for this picture on January 11, 1944.

We were set for a boy. The heartbeat was right for a boy. I had already picked out his name. I hadn't even considered a girl.

"What will we call her if it's a girl?" Margie asked while we waited together in the labor room. *"You know, we just might get a surprise."*

"Oh, why don't we call her Linda," I said offhandedly, confident we would have a boy.

Margie's pains were closer together now. The baby was about to arrive. I walked along holding her hand as the attendants wheeled her into the delivery room.

"Come on in or get out," the white-coated doctor demanded as he saw me hesitating in the doorway.

"Can I come in?" I asked, startled by the possibility.

"Sure, C'mon."

I was fascinated by the miracle of our baby's birth. I held Margie's hand the entire time. *"I think I've seen God do something in front of my eyes,"* I thought to myself when I saw the baby delivered and observed another life coming from my wife. The idea that God had given us our baby filled my heart with joy.

Fraser and I were still together. We took advantage of the Air Corps policy regarding brothers. So he was assigned to Pecos too. But Linda's birth created the first hint of a separation between us. Linda, Margie and I were now a family unit. He realized we had something he didn't and that started a drift in our relationship.

The gap widened when Fraser got orders assigning him to India. It was the first time in our lives we had ever been split up. I could have gone too. But I didn't want to go overseas. I had a reason for wanting to remain stateside—I had a family now.

Yet that wasn't to continue. It wasn't long afterwards that I got orders for overseas duty as well. We sold off our furniture in Pecos, loaded up the remnants in the car and drove back to Los Angeles. Leaving our baby daughter with Margie's parents, we boarded an airliner for a relocation center in Nashville, Tennessee. The plan.

was for Margie to stay with me in Nashville until I received my overseas assignment. That way we could be together until the last minute.

But El Paso was as far as Margie could go. In those days military personnel had the priority over civilian travel, and so she had to give up her seat on the plane. We knew I was going overseas, but we didn't know when or *if* I'd be coming home. So I got off the plane too, and we spent the fleeting night in El Paso.

The next morning I saw her off on the train. I was in tears as the cars pulled away from the station. Margie's face was pressed against the window. Tears were on her face and the glass. The depot must have been filled with people—but I saw no one but my beloved. It was so painful to separate. The completeness of our lives together was glorious and now we were torn apart by the war.

My orders were for India too. On the way our four-engine troop transport landed at Abadan, a refining and shipping center on the Shatt al Arab River in southwestern Iran. It was the middle of the night yet the temperature was 120 degrees outside. The runways were so hot you could fry an egg on them.

Just for a lark, one of the crew members took an egg and actually *did* fry it!

The next leg of the flight took me on to Karachi, at that time an important city of India, but now the capital of Pakistan. The allies had a replacement center in Karachi. Most service personnel were shuttled through the bustling city, a major stop on military flights between Europe and the Orient.

Some thirty officers were in the assembly room awaiting assignments shortly after I arrived. *"We need three pilots for Jamshedpur,"* the briefing officer announced mechanically one morning. No one seemed to want the assignment. So he arbitrarily pointed out three who were to go. *"We also need two for Delhi,"* he said looking down at his clipboard.

Ah, New Delhi! That was a name I recognized. *"I'll take that,"* I replied, raising my hand impulsively.

The officer peered at me over the top of the clipboard, a knowing smile on his face... *"You wouldn't be looking for a spot, would you Lovett?"*

"Not really, sir. The name just sounded familiar, that's all."

I wasn't sure what the assigning officer meant by a "spot," but I gathered from his voice it was a choice assignment. Indeed it was. Delhi was the capital of India and general headquarters for the CBI, the China-Burma-India theatre of war.

The airbase to which I was assigned existed primarily to accommodate generals. It was a plush place. Also a "per diem" station, which meant I got an extra $6.00 a day just for being there. The British had been there for decades so the facilities were nice. My quarters were wired with 220 outlets. I had a restful bed complete with mosquito netting, a large electric overhead fan to keep the humid air circulating and an electric phonograph.

The place even came equipped with an Indian servant by the name of Maloom. His family had been servants for generations. They considered it an honor to serve—especially foreigners. Never in my life had I seen service or devotion such as Maloom's.

Most of the servants were paid four annas a day. That was about eight cents. Though we were warned not to overpay our bearers, I gave Maloom six annas (twelve cents). He was worth it. His service included such things as walking seven miles into town simply to get a block of ice that I might have a cold drink. He even slept in the doorway of my basha so that a wandering cobra would encounter him first.

In spite of all the comforts of home, I didn't feel at home. My heart was back in California with my wife and baby. I wrote Margie every day, sometimes more often. She wrote equally as much. In one of her letters she mentioned going to church and singing in the choir. I was glad for her. I knew it would fill a void in her life while I was overseas—of course, I wanted none of it for myself.

India was a strange land to me, so full of superstition, ignorance and poverty. Most Westerners had difficulty understanding the Indian ways. The people weren't supposed to throw their babies into the sacred rivers of the Ganges and Jumna as sacrifices—but they did. Bodies often floated up on sandbars producing buzzards so thick they'd blot out the sun.

Flying operations were occasionally suspended because the buzzards posed such a hazard. We had pilots killed and planes lost when a buzzard would go through the windshield. When a "Wingram" warned us of buzzards, we took the communication seriously.

Margie's picture on the mantle kept my heart at home (top).
Little Linda showed everyone daddy's picture, as she and
Margie awaited my return from India (bottom).

SCENES FROM INDIA: I posed for Margie in front of the headquarters sign (top left), and near my basha at New Delhi (top right). The Taj Mahal at Agra (bottom left), and a woman teaching her son to beg at my bus window (bottom right) show the extreme living conditions.

Since I piloted a general's aircraft, I got to see a good bit of the country. In spite of its mystery and beauty, India has a seamy side. In Calcutta I saw garbage piles fifty feet high behind our hotel. People lived in those piles of garbage. They tunneled into the trash to make warm nests for themselves. The heat of fermenting garbage warmed their bodies at night.

People died in the streets of the big cities. Sometimes they'd stay there awhile. More than once I had to step over a corpse while walking down the street. I found people living and dying in unbelievable conditions, often surviving in nothing more than a doorway.

Many Indians were afraid to kill animals or even the smallest of insects for fear they possessed the soul of an ancestor. Even worse, they revered these creatures as gods. It was common to see pilgrims wearing cloths over their mouths to keep from accidentally inhaling an insect and killing it.

I won't forget a funny sight in a shop in downtown Delhi. A white bull had sauntered into the place knocking valuable merchandise from the shelves. Cups and pottery crashed to the floor. Teak wood boxes, ivory carvings, brassware and delicate works of art tumbled against one another in the melee.

The shop owner bowed himself low before the clumsy creature, and in a reverential manner tried to coax the bull out the door—at the same time daring to do nothing that would offend this god. I was told India had 150 million such gods.

Another time, in Delhi, I noticed a Brahman, a Hindu of the highest caste, standing on a street corner, staring directly into the sun. Since it was midday and hot, it seemed to me the man would injure his eyes if he didn't stop.

The street was a blur of activity, yet no one seemed to take notice of him. I was curious. *"What's this guy doing?"* I asked a passing Indian, who fortunately spoke English.

The man looked briefly at the Brahman and then turned to me, *"Oh, he's worshipping the sun."*

I was astounded by such a thing. But I found myself making another request of the gentleman. *"Would you ask him a question for me? Find out why he worships the sun instead of the One Who made the sun?"* That was a strange thing for me to ask, when I myself was baffled by thoughts about the One Who made the sun.

The man returned to the Brahman, pointed to me and then asked the question. The Hindu priest suddenly turned toward me. His dark eyes flashed angrily. His fists clenched.

"You'd better leave," the passerby advised excitedly, *"or this Brahman will give you some real trouble."*

I pushed through the small crowd that quickly gathered to see what the American officer was up to. I shook my head at the foolishness of the situation. *"How stupid can a person get. Imagine worshipping the sun when you know it didn't make itself!"* It seemed to me even a pagan should know better than that. *"Why not worship the One Who made it?"*

None of the Indian religions seemed to have any answers for the questions of life. Everywhere you looked you saw the fruits of those religions—disease, starvation, poverty. Why would anyone in his right mind want that? Ah, but if you didn't have that, what would you worship?

Inside of me was that haunting struggle for truth and reality. I was feeling things I couldn't explain, things I'd been feeling for a long time. Everything around me, everything that happened to me seemed to aggravate the questions struggling within me from my youth. *"Who am I?"* I continued to ask myself. *"Why am I here?"*

CHAPTER FIVE

"Margie, I've Found Out..."

Fraser was up in the mosquito-infested Assam Valley, a region in northeastern India between Bengal, Burma and the Himalaya Mountains, flying C-46 cargo aircraft "over the hump" into China. The region was mostly jungle with many steep hills and high mountains. Its rainfall was often six hundred inches a year, the world's heaviest.

The forward outposts had primitive conditions—tent cities, poor sanitary facilities, crude field kitchens. It was easy to get sick. Fraser contacted some Asian type of dysentery and couldn't shake it. He was sick continually.

General Terry was my boss. I spoke to him of the pos-

76

sibility of having Fraser transferred down to New Delhi. *"Consider it done,"* he replied without a moment's thought.

It was a thrill for me when my brother stepped off the plane. I was shocked at how thin and emaciated he was. I rushed up and threw my arms around him.

"Hi," he announced, *"Boy, am I glad to be here."*

We got him moved in right next door to my basha. For the next few months he did more fattening than flying! That was no problem since we had the best of everything in New Delhi. And did he need it.

Several months later, our whole outfit was in an outdoor theater one night, watching a Clark Gable movie when abruptly the film stopped. Lights came on. Conversation buzzed. *"What's going on?"* different ones shouted.

An announcement came over the loudspeaker—*"The Japanese have asked for peace terms!"*

Pandemonium broke loose. G.I.'s were instantly throwing things into the air—pillows, hats, chairs, anything they could get their hands on. It developed into a wild fracas before order could be restored.

Almost immediately, bases started closing down operations, resulting in personnel being returned to the states. Eventually my name came up. I was eager to get back to my wife and daughter. My brother stayed behind in Delhi inheriting my old job for a brief time. Then he shipped home too.

Fraser and I were so glad to be together again as we posed in the cockpit (above), and in front of the general's DC-3 named "Flyspeck" (below). In the background is an Indian temple, adjacent to the flying field.

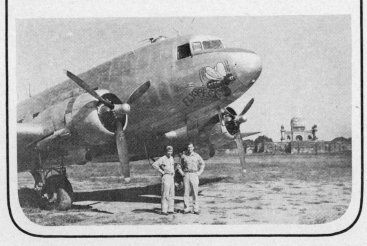

The return trip took me home by boat. I boarded the tour ship, Santa Rosa, at Karachi, traveled through the Suez Canal, crossed the Mediterranean and ploughed through the stormy Atlantic during the blustery month of December.

It was a thrilling experience when the Statue of Liberty first came into sight in New York harbor. Even more glorious was being united with my family in California.

It was glorious to get back to Margie after my tour of duty in India.

With the end of the war, price controls were lifted and the telephone started ringing with people wanting to buy the commercial properties we had purchased. Lots for which we had paid only a thousand dollars were suddenly selling for fifty thousand.

Prices were spiraling daily. People bidding continually.

Fraser and I agreed we'd wait for the right price on each lot before we'd sell, or unless we needed cash for a current building project. There were days when I walked around with twenty or thirty thousand dollars in my pocket before making a trip to the bank to deposit it.

In one year's time, we grossed $880,000!

Dad had taught us a healthy respect for money. One of his favorite expressions was *"take good care of your money and your money will take good care of you."* So my brother and I came to look on money as we would a piece of property. It was something to be exploited, not frittered away foolishly.

Besides selling off choice plots, I frequently bought property. Dad had also taught us how to search out tax titles to distressed properties. There seemed to be countless parcels being sold for nonpayment of taxes. I'd pay fifty dollars for a quit claim deed, get a judge to grant title to the property and end up with a clear piece of real estate.

That's essentially how I got land for our first home. With just two thousand dollars and Fraser's help, I put up a two-bedroom stucco house in West Los Angeles. In the rear, we constructed a comfortable garage apartment where Fraser and his newlywed wife lived.

If you look closely, you can see little Linda helping Fraser and me (in uniform) build our first home in West Los Angeles (top). When it was finished, the Lovett Brothers were still together. His garage apartment can be seen in the rear (bottom).

Fraser and I enjoyed building motels together. We took time our for a picture during construction (top); and were proud of the "Plantation Hotel," completed in Febuary 1948 (below).

It was fun working with my brother. Construction was always foremost in our plans and the Lovett Brothers embarked into building motels. It was natural for us to follow in the wake of our father's success. Our first project was a handsome 24-unit motel, which was so successful, we followed it with an elegant two-story colonial complex called "The Plantation Hotel."

Linda was growing up and Margie felt the need to get her into Sunday school. A Beverly Hills Presbyterian Church was not far, so that's where she went. I stayed home. I was typical of those parents who want for their children something they don't want for themselves.

One day, Margie casually asked me to go along. *"Sure,"* I responded, obviously suffering a lapse of memory. I was forgetting what had happened in that little church in Yuma during the war. But God wasn't forgetting. It was communion day again. Just as before, this pastor talked about the blood of Jesus. I felt as though he were talking directly to me. Tears cascaded from my eyes onto my clothes. The floor around me seemed wet with my weeping.

Afterwards the pastor walked over and tried to comfort me, but he didn't seem to know what to do or say. I hurt so inside, yet I was at a loss to explain what was wrong. Margie couldn't help.

At last, I regained my composure. Once more I walked red-eyed from an empty sanctuary. I couldn't stand to have people see me like that, so I waited until the crowd was gone.

"Margie, this is awful," I said driving home. *"I can't go through this again. Please don't ask me to go any more."*

My dear wife was silent. When the identical scene had happened in Yuma, she had agreed not to attend church. Now she was quiet. I could tell she was going through some kind of a struggle herself. That struggle would become more intense for her after reading Lloyd C. Douglas' book, "The Robe." That, plus comments made by Linda about her Sunday school lessons, were causing her to think seriously of her own needs.

Time has a way of changing things. For reasons unknown to me, my brother joined the Vermont Avenue Presbyterian Church. As far as I knew, he had no more interest in spiritual things than I did. Maybe he thought it would be good for business. I did feel the need to keep up with him, however, so I followed his example. I went before the church session to be examined, secretly purposing in my heart not to get involved in any of its "religious stuff." In this way I fortified myself against any recurrence of the embarrassing tears which plagued me previously.

Wayne Walbridge, a tall, friendly guy, was the church's business manager. He cornered me one day in the foyer of the sanctuary. *"CS, they're having a pastors' conference at Pacific Palisades next weekend,"* he announced breezily. *"How about going with me?"*

"A ministers' conference. What a bore." I thought to myself. *"The last thing in the world I could care about is going to a ministers' conference."* Yet outwardly I wanted to be nice to the fellow, so I gave him a polite

stall. *"Yeah, why don't you give me a call and we'll see?"*

"Great," he said, walking off quite pleased with himself.

Wait a minute! I couldn't believe what I had just done. I'd actually indicated an interest in a ministers' conference—me, the guy who couldn't handle a communion service. What had I done?

"Oh well, maybe he'll forget it," I told myself. *"And if he doesn't, I'll find some excuse for not going."*

Within a matter of days I had forgotten about the conference. Then the phone rang. *"This is Wayne,"* the voice announced. *"Remember we're going to the conference together. I have a couple of sleeping bags in the car. I'll be over in half an hour to pick you up. See you then."*

"Click." The phone went dead.

I stood there speechless. I didn't have a chance to make an excuse or anything. I hurried into the kitchen where Margie was baking some cookies for Linda.

"That was Wayne Walbridge. He says he's going to be here in 30 minutes to pick me up for that ministers' conference," I blurted in an unnerved tone of voice. *"I don't want to go to that thing. I'm gonna get out of here. You put him off when he arrives."*

But Margie was no help. *"Oh, it won't hurt you. Why don't you go?"* she said sweetly. *"They'll probably appreciate your being there."*

"But...," I stammered.

"O, c'mon, honey, don't disappoint Wayne. He's such a nice fellow. You never know. You might even enjoy it."

I melt easily under the spell of Margie's sweet influence. After that I didn't have the backbone to tell Wayne *"no."* Within minutes I was in Wayne's car headed toward Pacific Palisades and the ministers' conference. But there was no anticipation in my soul, believe me. I was set to suffer.

Some preacher who introduced himself as Bob Pierce was talking about hungry children in China as the conference began. *"They're lying in the streets covering themselves with newspapers,"* Pierce said intently. *"They have no food and nowhere to go."*

Various ministers followed Pierce to the platform. A number of them talked about missionary programs. Some preached. Others talked about prayer. I was miserable—bored stiff. I couldn't have cared less about all the stuff these people were discussing.

Finally a break came. It was intermission. Wayne walked off to chat with some friends. I found myself halfway back in the auditorium, seated in a hard-bottom chair carelessly leaning against the wall. I began rebuking myself in Laurel and Hardy fashion: *"How could you do it? Another fine mess you've gotten yourself into."*

As I was pondering my plight, my ears began to pick up on a conversation. My attention shifted from my distress to a group of the conference leaders standing a few feet away. They had been introduced as Bob Pierce, Harold Ockenga, Richard Halverson, Armin Gesswein and Robert Boyd Munger.

Their conversation, though private to them, was designed for me.

"If people only knew," one of the men was saying, *"all they have to do is talk to Jesus directly and He'll hear them."*

"Yeah," another agreed, *"you simply ask the Lord to come into your heart. That's all there is to it. There's no secret formula, no agonizing, no nothing."*

A third man put the final piece in place. *"The whole trick is asking Him in and letting Him make Himself real to you,"* he said. *"But people always try to make it complicated, when God means for it to be as simple as 'Lord Jesus come into my heart!' "*

"CLICK." The light went on.

I suddenly knew the answer to the big ache inside me. All those years of wondering. All I had to do was speak directly to Jesus and ask Him to come into my heart and make Himself real to me! Wow! The curtain was going up. What a great moment for C. S. Lovett!

The men walked back to the front of the auditorium totally unaware of the effect their words had on me. My brain was operating in overdrive now. Many of my experiences began flooding back into my mind—the questions and the doubts, the times my life had been spared supernaturally, the experience at the cemetary, crying in that church at Yuma, then crying in that church in Beverly Hills. It was all adding up!

"Why had I never heard this truth before?" That upset me. *"If it is really as simple as the news I'd just heard, why didn't someone tell me?"* It didn't make sense. *"Why didn't that pastor in Yuma tell me to ask Jesus into my heart? Didn't the Presbyterian know? And what about my parents, or my grandparents? Weren't they Christians?"*

As the realization was sweeping over me, I could hardly stand it. The information I had picked up was so vital, so basic—the key to life, actually. I wasn't sure I could hold inside what I was feeling. It seemed I'd explode if it didn't come out. One thing I knew—I had to get out of there and get home. I had to tell Margie what I'd discovered.

Wayne returned to where I was sitting. I don't know what he saw in my face, but he acted at once on my request. *"Wayne, I've got to get out of here. I've got to get home."*

"All right," he conceded. *"We can go right now if you want."* I knew he wasn't ready to leave, but he sensed something had happened in me.

He drove me back home. We hardly talked. I wanted Margie to be the first to hear. I'm not sure I even thanked him as I ran from the car and burst into the house shouting...*"Margie! Margie! I've found out what it's all about! Come here quick!"* I was half-crying, half-laughing—all at the same time.

Margie was drying her hands on a towel as she appeared in the kitchen doorway. *"Honey, what on earth... what are you so excited about!"* My gushing emotions caught her off guard.

"Just give me your hand and come here," I said, trying to keep the lid on my excitement.

I almost dragged her into the living room where I spewed out the conversation I had overheard. *"All we have to do is talk to Jesus,"* I assured her. *"He can hear us! He's waiting right now for us to invite Him into our hearts. And if we'll do that, He'll come in and prove himself to us."*

"Really, honey?" There was excitement in her voice now. The smile on her face indicated she was right with me.

"Yeah, honestly, that's all there is to it. It has nothing to do with church. It's just between us and Him—and we can do it right now!"

Margie was ready. Without another moment passing, we knelt together in the quiet of our living room and spoke directly to the Lord:

> *"Lord Jesus, we know this is the moment we've been waiting for. You are what we want. And if You want to come into our hearts, we open the door to You right now. We invite You to come in and be our personal Savior."*

The ceiling of the room seemed to open. It was like a gust of heavenly air sweeping our souls. Margie and I knew He had come into our hearts. We felt cleansed and free. I actually forgot where I was. Time was suspended. Finally we hugged each other tightly. Her eyes were washed with tears. The old longing in my heart was subsiding rapidly. The ache was completely gone. The sensation in my spirit was akin to that which I had enjoyed in a plane so often. But now it was my soul that had wings.

I had heard a lot about God. I had gone to Sunday school as a kid. Listened to radio programs with my stepfather. A lot of information had been stored inside me—unconsciously. But now at the age of 30—it all came alive! I felt as though I had shaken hands with God and He was glad to see me. It was the greatest thrill I'd ever known! It was glorious to be a Christian—*at last!*

For the first time in my life I felt a deep, inner peace. Of course I didn't have immediate answers to all the questions that had dogged my steps and stabbed my heart from time-to-time, but the tension between myself and God was gone. The war was over. Peace had been declared. I slept like a baby that night—free of the anguish and restlessness that had smoldered all those years. I knew my sins were *forgiven*. The answers would be coming, I sensed that. But praise God the big battle was over. Oh, what joy!

CHAPTER SIX

Answering The Call

The days following my conversion were filled with indescribable joy! The Holy Spirit seemed to delight in revealing Christ to me. I floated on a cloud, overwhelmed with the reality of Jesus' presence.

Then one day the Holy Spirit struck me with a tremendous thought:

GOD HAD ARRANGED FOR ME TO GROW UP WITHOUT A FATHER SO THAT HE COULD BE THE ONLY FATHER I'D REAL-LY KNOW!

I was twenty-one years old when I met C. A. Lovett. We didn't have a father-son relationship. That wasn't possible, since he was a stranger to me in many ways. Never once did he call me "*son*." So in no way did he fill the vacuum inside me.

But now that I had come to know the Lord, I found in Him Someone Who loved me enough to die for me. Then to realize that He lived inside me made the relationship so intimate. He could see me at my worst— and still love me. With that understanding, I rejoiced at finding MY OWN DEAR FATHER at last. I now had a Parent Who would take me as I was and help me become all that I could be. The void in my soul was *filled* by my Heavenly Father!

Since I didn't have to work at a nine-to-five job for a living, I could spend eight hours a day reading the Bible if I wanted to. And that's what Margie and I did. Our house had a cute breakfast nook with a bay window. We set the coffee pot in the middle of the table and began reading—all day. We were interrupted only by Linda's occasional demands. I also had no pressing construction projects.

Although I wasn't one to weep easily, I wept freely as I read, especially when I saw how God loved the wayward nation of Israel. I cried because I knew He loved me even more—and I was just as wayward.

Many of the things I'd heard in Sunday school now fell into place. My mind churned over and over as I read the Scriptures. The Holy Spirit seemed to open the Word to me. It was like my own personal Pentecost.

I couldn't get over God's love for me. Years before I

had stood in that shower feeling totally worthless. Now, in 1947, I found the Creator of the universe in love with me. To me the Bible was the Last Will and Testament of a Billionaire Relative Who had left me His inheritance. I was reading the will and the codicils. I was *the* heir.

Sometimes after reading eight hours, I still wanted more. I read until my eyes ached. Margie and I frequently went to bed and I'd pray for an hour after she'd fallen asleep. Nobody had to tell me to pray. I loved it. I was so excited over discovering the Lord, I couldn't stop talking to Him. Chatting with the eternal God as a personal Friend was a fascination and a compulsion. I couldn't get enough of Him.

Mother, Daddy and Linda—all saved and happy about it.

Several months passed. People frequently came to our home for Bible study. That was our passion now. We just sat around in a circle reading verses and talking about the mysteries of the Word as though that were the chief pleasure in life. I really didn't want to talk to people unless it was about the Lord or the Bible. It was a spiritual honeymoon!

One Sunday it was too late for us to get to the Presbyterian church on time. *"There's that little Baptist church over on La Cienega,"* Margie suggested over a last minute cup of coffee. *"Why don't we try it? It's only a few blocks away."*

The church was friendly but nothing special, neither was the pastor. But a few days later, I was shoveling sand and gravel into a cement mixer for a backyard patio— when up walked Leonard Prentice. *"I just came by to say hello and get acquainted,"* the friendly, bespectacled pastor announced warmly.

There was something about Prentice I liked, and I appreciated his visit. It was because of his visit that Margie and I went back often and finally joined the little church. How different it was going to church now— compared to before. I had a hunger to be with other Christians.

Pastor Prentice took an immediate interest in me, almost as if he saw something God could use. He began spending long hours with me every afternoon, pouring much of himself into me. He answered my complicated questions, taught me Old Testament history and loaded me down with books from his personal library. Before long, I was teaching the adult Sunday school class.

Throughout 1948 to 1951, we stayed at La Cienega

Baptist working with pastor Prentice and enjoying his coaching.

Leonard Prentice, the man who took me under his wing right after I was saved—and his wife Alice.

Dad's success was obviously rubbing off on his boys. It looked as if nothing could stop us in the construction business. The motels we had constructed were booming.

But I was troubled. I was continually running across Scriptures referring to rich people. *"It's harder for a rich man to get into heaven than a camel to go through the eye of a needle."* Everything I saw seemed to say, *"Watch out for wealth!"* I was beginning to think there was a penalty for being rich. With the way our business was headed, I was set to become extremely rich.

This conflict was brewing inside me, bothering me enough to send me to pastor Prentice. He tried to ease my distress. *"God needs millionaires, too,"* he said. But that didn't help. More and more I was sensing the call to forsake the way of wealth and serve the Lord.

Then one day he took me to visit Sarah Teasdale, an elderly woman who had been a long-time member at La Cienega Baptist. We hadn't been in this godly woman's home five minutes when she looked into my face and pointed a bony finger at me.

"Young man," she said firmly, *"The Holy Spirit says you're fighting the Lord. He wants to use you and you're resisting Him."*

"Ouch!" She put her finger on my sore spot. I suffered a tremendous reaction inside. I wanted to get out of there so badly. *"How could she have possibly known?"* I said to myself. As Leonard and I drove home in silence, the Spirit reminded me of the way Agabus warned the apostle Paul. Would I ignore the warning as he did?

I was having trouble with dreams. Almost every night I would dream about preaching. I'd see myself as a minister and it terrorized me. Many times I would cry out in the night and find myself sitting erect...covered with perspiration.

"What's wrong, dear?" My jerking movements would awaken Margie.

"I just had another one of those awful nightmares," I answered, wiping my face on the sleeve of my pajamas. *"I dreamed I was preaching."*

My concept of the ministry was a dismal one. Once two bachelor preachers had rented the upstairs apartment in mother's duplex. They were so poor they could scarcely pay the rent. They drove a rusted hulk. They could never afford new clothes. They seemed so sad all the time. Even in Tulare, the preachers I'd seen there looked the same. I couldn't think of anything *worse* than being a preacher!

On the other hand, I liked money. I also liked success. And that's what I now had at last. Fraser and I had pyramided our holdings and it was paying off—big. We were into large building projects with the promise of millions. Beyond that, with Fraser's skills and my ability to negotiate, there was no limit to what we could do.

Dad knew all that. He sensed it and frequently told us we could go as far as we wanted. He had already made his fortune. Now his dream was to watch his boys enjoy the same success. He was getting a big bang out of it. In fact, it was about all he had to live for.

Above all, I was fascinated with making money. I liked its power, the feeling it gave. I particularly liked the security it offered. Money seemed to be the key to everything.

I wanted to continue in the business and at the same time, experience the best of Christ. Yet, I felt this strange call, one I couldn't shake. To have that lady say what she did, putting it so bluntly, brought the matter to the surface. Needless to say, I didn't like it one bit. Once it was in the open like that, it was now something I had to reckon with.

Mother had moved from Los Angeles to Berkeley, California after Fraser and I had left home. Even though we had seen her on occasions, the atmosphere had been cold and strained. But after I had become a Christian, the ice was broken. Even though she hadn't talked to me much about Jesus before I was saved, mother had been a Christian for many years. My new relationship with the Lord produced a new relationship with her. She loved Jesus too.

During the time I was wrestling with the call to serve the Lord, Margie and I visited mother in Berkeley. With my stepfather, the four of us were seated around mother's kitchen table enjoying coffee and cake.

"You won't believe the project the Lovett Brothers are into now," I bragged to her.

"I never know what you boys are going to do next," she said, brushing off cake crumbs from the table. *"What is it this time?"*

"Fraser and I have pooled our assets and have gone in with C. A. to build a 450-unit motel including a cocktail bar, restaurant and pool at Adams and Figueroa in downtown Los Angeles. It's got to be a gold mine!"

"Cocktail bar? Gold mine?" she muttered.

98

"Yeah, isn't that fabulous!" I enthused.

Her eyes met mine and held me in a vise. *"Honey,"* she asked firmly, *"Don't you care anything about serving the Lord?"*

The lines on mother's face deepened. Her jaw was tight and rigid. I recognized the pain she felt. Without another word, she got up from the table and walked into the living room. The atmosphere was deathly still. Nobody said a word. For the second time the Holy Spirit spoke to me through a godly woman. Her question was like a sledgehammer breaking up my concrete-like resistance. In minutes, the whole load I was carrying gave way.

I ran into the living room, fell on my knees at her feet and buried my face in her lap, sobbing. *"You're right mother, you're right,"* I said tearfully. *"I don't care what it costs me. I'm going to serve the Lord. Everything else is second."*

For months I had been torn by indecision. I had labored under a heavy load of conviction. The suffering was so bad, I didn't see how going into the ministry could be any *worse*. When I got off my knees, there was no wavering in my mind. Everything was settled. I knew what I had to do. There would be no peace until I did.

Margie and I drove the eight hours back to Los Angeles. I hurriedly called my dad and asked him to come over. That night after supper he arrived. We went into the living room to talk. Dad took the big easy chair. I knelt down on the floor beside him—much as I had done with mother hours before. He looked as if he expected something monumental from me.

"Dad, I'm not going to be able to work with you and Fraser anymore." I couldn't think of any way to soften the blow.

"What did you say?" he replied, sitting upright in his chair.

"I can't work with you anymore," I repeated, *"I'm going to serve the One Who died for me. I've committed myself to serve Christ."*

"Wha-what-wha-wha," he stuttered in disbelief.

"I'm going to give up the building business," I said resolutely. *"I've been called to serve the Lord, and from the misery I've already suffered, I know I can't do anything else. I know it's a shock to you, but believe me dad, I can't do anything else."*

He shook his head. *"You can't mean it. You'd better think about this some more. It's got to be a hasty decision on your part. No, I won't hear of it."*

I smiled. I didn't really expect him to understand. *"No, dad, I've thought about this for a long time. In fact, I've even fought it. It's something I just have to do."*

"But what about all this?" he mumbled, gesturing over a set of blueprints for the new motel complex spread across a coffee table. *"You've got all your assets in this. So has Fraser. What about that?"*

That's what it boiled down to. We'd come to the bottom line, *money*. From deep within me came that grace only the Holy Spirit can give.

"TAKE IT," I said freely. I suddenly felt the wealth of heaven was mine.

"Take it?" he exploded. *"You can't be serious. Everything you've made is invested in this project. You'll be wiped out!"*

"But I am serious, dad," I answered calmly, smiling. *"I want you to take it."*

There was nothing dad could do. His shoulders dropped with disappointment. I had been his favorite. Now here I was breaking up the team. He figured he would spend his last days coaching his boys and watching them become millionaires. When he went out the door he knew his dream was shattered. There wasn't much left for him now.

My father couldn't understand my decision. He was a scoffer—always making fun of Christianity. He'd been exposed to the gospel as a child. His mother had attempted to drill it into him. *"Cram it down my throat,"* were his words. He rebelled. To this day he wanted no part of it.

My brother and I were still close. We loved each other. That would never change. We had worked beautifully as a team. Yet, when I made the decision to leave the corporation, he continued to work with my father. There was no reason for my brother to accept my call as his. So Fraser and Sam went different ways...after all those years together.

The price of my decision was heavy. The loss of my fortune and my earthly father were nothing compared to the loss of my brother. That was the most expensive part. Answering the call of God was now the primary thing in my life. Nothing was more important than obeying my Heavenly Father!

CHAPTER SEVEN

"You're Going To School!"

I was involved in a "love affair"—with the Lord. I thrilled to the new found intimacy with Him, an intimacy which I had longed for all those years. Since He lived within me, seeing me at my worst yet loving me still, I felt completely at home in His presence.

That made for a fabulous relationship. No pretense, no religious language. I could be myself with Him. It was great having the Maker of heaven and earth for my very own Father and Friend.

After reading and studying sections of the Bible on prophecy, Margie and I discovered God's plan for the world. We prayed every day for the Holy Spirit to show us exactly how we fitted into that plan. We wanted to be available for whatever He might have in mind for us, therefore we decided not to raise a big family.

However, we were concerned about raising Linda as an only child. That concern took us to our knees. The answer came on September 20, 1950. We named her Donna Lee. She was such a special gift from the Lord, bringing much joy and pleasure into our home. We felt Donna was one of God's unique blessings to us because of our strong commitment to Him.

A proud papa holding Donna Lee, our special gift from the Lord. Seven-year-old Linda was happy to have a sister.

Pastor Prentice was one of the first with whom I shared my decision to leave the construction business. The Lord really used him to guide me during my early days as a Christian. He was thrilled for me and had an immediate suggestion. *"I think we're going to have to get you started in school,"* he said thoughtfully.

"Go to school!" Ugh, I didn't like that idea. I had already spent better than three years in a two-year college. The thought of starting again was anything but appealing. I hadn't done too well anyway, struggling along with C's and D's because of my interest in girls. *"Is it really necessary?"* I protested.

By this time, Leonard had begun letting me help with his Sunday sermons. We'd talk about various passages of Scripture and I'd volunteer my opinions. Later I'd hear some of my ideas coming from the pulpit. I liked that. In time, he asked me to preach.

But after hearing me struggle through my first sermon, brother Prentice was even more positive. *"No question about it,"* he announced firmly, *"you're going to school!"*

In the end I agreed. It did seem like the next logical step to wherever God was leading me.

It was February, 1951. California Baptist Theological Seminary was located in downtown Los Angeles. Pastor Prentice actually drove me down in his car to get me enrolled. He knew the dean. I was aced back into school almost like a shoehorn sliding an uncooperative foot into a ready shoe.

The seminary moved from downtown Los Angeles to Covina, about twenty miles east, after I had been there one semester. Margie and I decided to sell the cozy little house we'd built with our own hands. It had been the very place we asked Christ into our hearts, and where we had had great times in Bible study groups. The move tugged at the strings of my heart, and Margie had tears in her eyes the day we and our two girls packed up and drove away.

We settled in our new home in Covina, and I was ready for my second semester.

Payson Gregory, a tall, "bean pole" guy who spoke in machine gun sentences, was one of the new friends I made at school. Payson had a wife and two kids and was struggling through seminary like a lot of others.

But he liked to talk with the Lord in a personal fashion as I did. Thus we developed a close friendship on our knees. The school had a tiny prayer chapel where we spent two or three hours daily chatting with the Lord in prayer. Our prayer times in that chapel were more like conferences with Jesus. No formality. No particular order. It was as though Jesus were right there, with the three of us enjoying each other. Our special request was that He would use us.

Payson was always kidding. He had a wry sense of humor. He saw the funny side of life. That made him a good balance for me, since I tended to be overly serious about things. We became close brothers in the Lord.

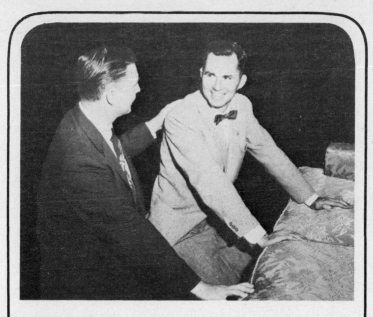

Where it all began—C. S. Lovett and Payson Gregory on their knees.

After moving to Covina, I was without a church home. So was Payson. I guess it was only natural for him to offer a solution. *"Why don't we start one?"* he half-suggested, half-asked one day after a prayer session.

"You're kidding," I responded, thinking of Payson's usual manner.

"No, I'm serious," he answered. *"I'll betcha there are plenty of people in our neighborhood who'd join if we asked them. All we need is a place to meet. Why don't we give it a try?"*

Several afternoons we—Payson, myself and a few seminary students—knocked on doors. Payson had been right. There were people interested in attending a Baptist church. We'd heard the Baldwin Park Woman's Club was going to be available, so we located Mrs. Katie Elder who handled its rental.

"You can have the auditorium for ten dollars a Sunday," she explained. *"That includes the chairs, the pulpit stand and the lights. All we ask is that you clean up and put the chairs away before you leave."*

"It's a deal," I said, always quick to recognize a bargain.

Once we had rented the woman's club, we went back door-to-door notifying people about our first meeting. From the start, people responded to services at the woman's club. Before long, Baldwin Park Baptist Church, as we called ourselves, had a packed house each Sunday. People liked the services, told others and the crowds grew.

I enjoyed preaching. It gave me a unique opportunity to learn new things in seminary during the week and then preach them on Sundays from the pulpit. I learned rapidly because I was working with things I was studying.

Margie was a big help. She taught a Sunday school class and did the church bulletin on a mimeograph machine in the garage. She also created a nice environment in the home for me to study. Our home was a place of tranquility, peace and joy in the Lord—a great help in attending school and pastoring the church.

Our family in front of our home in Covina (above). The Baldwin Park Woman's Club provided a place for the church to meet. It was my first pastorate (below).

California Baptist was a rather liberal seminary. Pastor Prentice, a conservative, wanted me to attend the school because of its academic integrity. He knew I'd gain excellent skills with which to work. In short, I'd be properly equipped for the Lord's service.

Yet, because of Prentice's influence and his long hours of training, I had become a strict biblicist, a dyed-in-the-wool conservative. Because the school was liberal, I was headed for conflict almost from my first day there.

Dr. C. I. Scofield's Bible and writings had made a deep impression on me. I had practically memorized everything he wrote, using the Scriptures to back my positions. As far as I was concerned, even though it was extreme, there was little difference between C. I. Scofield and the Holy Spirit.

The Lord had given me a nimble mind. Often I would go to the blackboard to demonstrate my theological position. I argued my points vocally—at times, rather heatedly. Whenever the class was thrown open for questions, my hand was the first to go up. Many times my views were at odds with what the professors were teaching.

My approach tended to "put down" a few teachers. Some simply replied, *"you may be right,"* just to keep the class going. Ofttimes, when I would launch into one of my presentations, students closed their books. They knew what to expect. Seldom did the professor ever get around to the lesson. The bell would ring before we had completed our discussion.

I guess it was natural for me to react against the

teachers. I was thirty-five years old. I had been successful in business and was accustomed to wheeling and dealing. Certainly I was used to having my own way. With the weight of Scripture behind me, I wasn't intimidated by men of higher education. Of course, I could have been sweeter about it. But God was only starting to knock the rough edges off of C. S. Lovett.

The conflicts continued. But one day, months later, in a class on systematic theology, the professor, Dr. James Jauncey, backed me into a corner.

The issue centered around the death of Jesus. With Dr. Jauncey's permission, I went to the blackboard to present my position visually. The class grew still as I explained my concepts. My argument grew heated for I was sure I was right.

Dr. Jauncey, a lanky Australian with a strong accent, interrupted with a question that proved beyond a shadow of a doubt that I was wrong.

I was stunned for a moment. I hadn't explored *that* possibility. I had no answer on the tip of my tongue.

"I GUESS YOU'RE RIGHT AND I'M WRONG," I mumbled at last. I had never said anything like that before—certainly not aloud before a class.

The students broke into hearty applause. They'd never heard C. S. Lovett admit to being wrong before. They heard him debate all over the campus. A few teachers even hated to see him coming for fear of getting into an argument.

When the class period ended, I just sat there pondering what had happened. For C. S. Lovett to admit he could be wrong was like reversing the Colorado River. Students filed past me. Some patted me on the back. One or two shook my hand. A couple had tears in their eyes. To see God (for that's Who it really was) humble the defiant debater had an unusual impact on them.

Being wrong was a new experience for me. It stunned me. I wondered if I were wrong about this, what else might I be wrong about? *"Maybe I don't know everything after all,"* I considered.

Dr. Jauncey, a professor with fifteen earned degrees, was kind enough not to rub in his victory. He wisely understood what was happening. He waited a day or so before asking me to lunch.

"You know, Lovett," he said encouragingly, *"you have fantastic ideas."*

"Really? I'm beginning to wonder," I replied, not quite so sure of myself now.

"I think so."

"You say that after I had to back down in class?"

"Don't let that bother you," he said comfortingly. *"That was a wonderful experience for you. It can open the door of knowledge, if you'll let it. The person who has to be right every time, never learns. He's so locked into his own thinking, even God can't get through to him."*

"Hmmmmm," did that give me something to chew on. I was one who always had to be right.

Then he added a caution. *"I believe you're a little*

112

ahead of your time, however. You're going to find that not everyone is ready for you and your ideas."

"I think I'm beginning to find that out."

Satisfied he had gotten to me at last, he broadened into a wide grin, *"But I know the Holy Spirit is showing you many things and He is going to use you in a powerful way."*

Dr. Jauncey's encouragement meant a great deal. The situation in his classroom proved to be a turning point for me. Instead of trying to press my position all the time, refusing to consider other viewpoints, I opened up and began to listen. My learning rate went up dramatically.

In the process, the Lord blasted me from the rigid system to which I had bound myself—setting my mind and my spirit free! What a relief it was. I found it could even be FUN TO BE WRONG! That was a shift. It made a big difference in the way I handled myself around the other students and the professors.

There were immediate dividends, too. I was asked to teach several classes at seminary and was frequently used as a chapel speaker. It was nice to be useable. C. S. Lovett was a lot nicer fellow with his defensive thorns knocked off.

Still there were aspects of my Christian experience that seemed to bother some people. Never was that more evident than during my ordination proceedings. I

113

needed ordination to shift my military status from that of pilot to Air Force Chaplain. If I were returned to duty, I wanted to go back as a servant of the Lord.

Pastor Prentice was still at La Cienega Baptist and very active in the Conservative Baptist Association. He promised to sponsor me before an ordination council, a group of pastors and delegates who would examine my views on doctrine and practice.

As the examination began, several of the pastors shifted uncomfortably in their chairs when I talked of my views of God and Jesus Christ. I spoke of my intimate relationship with the Lord—enjoying Him as a person, laughing with Him, driving in the car and having Him find me a parking spot.

The men of the cloth reacted strangely to the fact that I took God as a personal Friend. Somehow in their minds I was bringing God down from His lofty position in glory to the level of human beings walking around on earth. This was really my point. To me, God wasn't off somewhere wandering around the portals of heaven. He was with me, in me. I didn't see how His omnipresence made Him any less God.

The preachers didn't agree. *"You're humanizing God,"* one of them complained. Most nodded agreement.

Freddie Lewis, an evangelist dressed in a bright sport coat and slick-backed hair, was the most vocal on the council. *"I've heard enough,"* he declared, standing to his feet. *"I think we should stop these proceedings right now. I'm ready to vote."*

Lewis was ruled out of order and the committee

114

moved to the next question. My ordination was hotly debated but, in the end, the council agreed to recommend it.

Dr. Robert Dennis and Rev. Leonard Prentice, representing the Conservative Baptist Association of Southern California, officiated my ordination.

I could understand how the preachers might stumble over my concepts on the local church and hell. They were new ideas and naturally brought some opposition. But I couldn't understand their hot reaction to my personal enjoyment of the Lord.

That's the way Jesus had revealed Himself to me. I had had no earthly father. Thus, when I discovered the

Lord as my Heavenly Father, it was only natural for Him to become everything I had longed for in an earthly father. That's why our relationship was never stuffy or formal. I called Him *"Dad,"* and we had long sessions together on a father and son basis.

To me, it was pure delight to have a father who was so rich and famous and took such pleasure in me. I didn't see Him as a God to be feared, but as a Father Who loved me and wanted us to have the most intimate fellowship possible.

Even in seminary, I was given an "F" for preaching a message in class one day entitled, "Poor God." My professor was offended by my suggestion that our God has needs which only we can fill, and that there is a place for believers to minister to the Lord. He was particularly upset when I said we should take good care of Him because He is the only God we have.

"Lovett, I hope you don't teach things like that from your own pulpit," he scolded. *"That message is in extremely bad taste."*

Of course I didn't feel that way at all. The joy of having a real Father at last was simply overwhelming for me. The thrill of having the word *"Father,"* on my lips told me I was on the right track. So I determined to bring as many people as I could into this personal relationship with the Lord. To me it was the heartbeat of Christianity.

CHAPTER EIGHT

A Plan For Reaching Lost Souls

"Street preaching" was one of the practical activities required of seminary students. A teacher from the school would take us to nearby towns to share our faith on the streets. Most of the passers-by paused and looked at us, then walked on. Sometimes a group would gather to listen for a time. But to me it seemed a clumsy way to get the job done. The poor results made me feel even more dissatisfied with such an approach.

I had heard lots of preaching before I was saved. My stepdad listened to gospel radio programs every evening when I was a teen-ager. I wasn't saved through any of that preaching. Coming to Christ as I did made me realize it took something MORE DIRECT. It seemed to me that people should be confronted with CHRIST ALIVE!

It burned me to hear people talk about Jesus as though He were a character from the Bible, when I knew Him to be alive, eager to get acquainted with all who'd like to know Him. Because of my personal relationship with Him, I felt Christianity was essentially personal.

"Let's go out on the streets," was a continual suggestion from Payson. But he didn't mean preaching. He meant approaching people and talking to them about Jesus, man-to-man. I was eager to go since it gave me a chance to speak with others about Jesus the way I knew Him. I was still rankling over the clumsy way I had come to the Lord. I knew there had to be a better way to go about it.

In those days, evangelicals were using a method of soul-winning that consisted of quoting verses to an unbeliever that showed why he should put his faith in Jesus. The unbeliever would give back his reasons for not accepting Christ. Then the Christian would counter with another verse from the Bible. Essentially it was a technique of using verses to answer excuses offered by the unsaved.

I think it would be fair to describe it as the "debate-method" of winning souls.

As far as I could see, people needed to face the fact that Jesus was a LIVING PERSON. That way the unbeliever was confronted by Him and not just another zealous Christian.

My first attempts to express this on the street were clumsy. I stopped people saying bluntly, *"Hey, did you know Jesus is alive. If you don't believe me, ask Him. He's right here. Talk to Him and you'll get the thrill of your life.''* They got a shock all right—me.

My boldness frightened most people. They didn't want to talk to me.

I tried softening the approach a bit. *"The Lord loves you,"* I began saying to people. *"He loves you enough to die for you and He wants to give you the gift of eternal life. All you have to do is open your heart to Him and tell Him you want Him."*

But people didn't seem to be ready for that either. *"I've heard that before,"* they would say nonchalantly and walk away.

I was mystified. I couldn't understand why they didn't want Jesus when He was only a word away. Their reaction baffled me. I knew Him to be such a fabulous Person, One ready to fill and thrill any heart that would receive Him. I enjoyed my own "love affair" with Him so much, I wanted everybody to get in on the blessing.

So compelling was the urge to share Jesus, I remained undaunted by my initial failures. I plugged along, continuing to witness on the streets. But somehow, my approach lacked authority. Eventually I began taking out a small pocket New Testament and opening it in front of people while talking with them. They seemed to recognize the Book. When I'd point to a Bible verse, it seemed to have an effect on them. Yet, we weren't getting the result I believed possible.

Payson and I returned to the prayer chapel one night after failing to win anybody on the streets. Some people had even reacted badly to our presentation.

"We must be doing something wrong," I offered.

"Maybe we're coming at it the wrong way," Payson speculated.

"In what way, do you think?"

"Well, I wonder if the news we're laying on these people isn't too much for them," he said. *"You know, we're practically telling them they're sinners and on the way to hell. That's a lot to handle, don't you think?"*

"You could be right," I said thoughtfully. *"Yes, we've got to soften our approach. What's more, it seems God has to give us some kind of a plan. There's too much trial and error in what we're doing. There's got to be a better way."*

For weeks following, we prayed specifically asking the Holy Spirit for direction. We continued having problems presenting Christ on the streets but we never let up in our prayers. *"Father, we know you have a plan for us,"* was our constant affirmation. By faith, we expected Him to reveal it to us.

One day between classes, I drove home for a bite of lunch. Carol Olson, a long-time friend of Margie's, was visiting. After downing a sandwich and milk, I walked into the living room where the girls were chatting.

Impulsively I began talking with Carol. *"You know,"* I smiled, *"in all the time we've been friends there's something I've never asked you."*

"Oh, what's that?"

"Are you interested in spiritual things?" I asked, not really knowing what to say, yet sensing the Holy Spirit was leading me.

120

"Oh sure, I've always been interested in religion," she came back.

"Have you ever thought of becoming a Christian?"

Carol looked surprised. *"Well, I...I think I am a Christian,"* she replied.

"If someone were to ask you what is a Christian, what would you say?" I continued, aware now of the direct leading of the Lord.

"That's easy," she enthused. *"It's someone who goes to church and lives a good moral life."*

"It's true a Christian DOES those things," I agreed, *"but what IS a Christian?"*

The puzzled look was back on Carol's face. *"Well, perhaps I'm not too sure,"* she admitted. *"Why don't you tell me."*

"If it's okay with you, I'd like to read four verses of Scripture that give the right answer," I said.

She nodded her agreement. I read the four verses explaining how: "all have sinned and come short of the glory of God" (Romans 3:23); "the wages of sin is death" (Romans 6:23); "but to as many as received Him, to them gave he power to become the sons of God" (John 1:12); "behold I stand at the door and knock..." (Revelation 3:20).

"Jesus never forces Himself on people. He wants them to want Him and tell Him so. Have you ever done this?" I asked softly.

121

"No, *not really*," she answered, rather surprised at herself.

"*The Lord is waiting to come into your heart right now*," I affirmed. "*Will you open the door? Will you invite Him in?*"

"*Oh, yes,*" she said tearfully. She was ready.

Leading her gently, I bowed my head. "*Follow me and we'll pray together.*"

Dear Lord Jesus—I confess that I am a sinner—and I here and now open the door of my heart—I invite You to come in—I now put my trust in You—as my personal Savior. Amen."

When she lifted her head, she knew what a Christian was. She was now one herself.

Carol Olson and Margie, like sisters since the fifth grade—now sisters in the Lord!

The missing link had been added. I knew the Lord had put those questions in my mind. Here was a plan directly from the Holy Spirit. The approach was so easy. I couldn't wait to give Payson the news.

Instantly we began reaping a harvest of souls with this technique. One Friday night the manager of a theater in Covina even chased us from the front of his movie house. We were winning all his potential movie-goers to the Lord and they were turning around to go back home.

On another occasion, Payson and I were invited to a large estate in San Marino, a wealthy Los Angeles sub-urb. Some seventy-five kids were in the house for a church outing. We'd been invited by a woman who had heard about our soul-winning success and who had been working as an advisor to these teen-agers for years.

I spoke for a few minutes, dealing essentially with the three approach questions and explaining how simple it was to invite Jesus into your heart. Then Payson and I stood back-to-back, with the youngsters forming two lines waiting to be saved. There was no confusion, no mumbo-jumbo. It was all crystal clear. Every kid in the house—all seventy-five of them—made clear cut decisions and invited Jesus into their hearts. They knew exactly what they were doing and why.

As Payson and I were driving home in the car, I re-flected on the way I came to the Lord. How different this was; so clear cut, so simple, so easy. Now I knew why the Lord, in His wisdom, dealt with me as He did. It was because He intended to use my burden to bring forth a plan that made soul-winning easy.

The Holy Spirit confirmed the power of the plan constantly at the jails and at L. A. County General Hospital where I worked with the chaplain's office. Rarely was there ever a time when I didn't lead ten or fifteen people to the Lord during a jail or hospital visit. As the days went by, the skill became even sharper. The Holy Spirit was ever revealing ways to improve the technique.

One day at the hospital, I picked up my visitation cards at the office and started on my rounds. As I checked in at a nurses' station, a grim-faced senior nurse gave me some advice.

"When you go in there," she said, nodding toward the ward entrance, *"you better skip the woman in the first bed. We just had to pull a man out of her bed a few minutes ago. She's in no mood to talk with anybody, especially a preacher."*

"Well, we'll see what the Lord has to say about that," I said smiling.

Before opening the door of the ward, I paused for a word with the real Soul-Winner. *"Lord, how would You have me deal with a woman like this? I know You already have an answer, so Lord Jesus, take over and speak through me."*

I turned toward the first bed screened by a long, white, pull-around curtain. *"I'm from the chaplain's office,"* I announced innocently, *"but I don't suppose you'd want to talk with me."*

124

"Who says I don't!" the woman shot back in a whiskey-soaked voice.

The light went on in my spirit. Ah ha, here was the approach...tell the woman what she doesn't want and she'll respond by saying she does.

"Well, I'm here to talk about the things of the Lord," I said, walking up beside the bed. *"I'm sure you don't want to hear about that kind of thing."*

"Who says I don't!" she repeated.

"Okay, then I'm going to read you four verses of Scripture." I read the passages and concluded, *"Now the Lord's knocking at the door of your heart but He won't come in without an invitation. You have to ask Him. I'm sure you wouldn't want to do that."*

"Yeah, I can if I want to, can't I?" She was a little softer now.

"Okay then, just bow your head and invite Him into your heart." Briefly I led her to get her started.

Then suddenly she was praying on her own. In fact, praying loudly. *"Lord, I've been such a sinner,"* she cried, tears drenching her face. *"I've made a mess of my life. If You can do anything with it, it's Yours. Please come into my heart and be my Savior."*

In the next bed was a black woman who had been attacked on the street the night before. She was a mass of cuts and bruises. *"I want Jesus too,"* she pleaded, rising up on one elbow.

I didn't have to repeat the whole plan with her. She'd

heard the other woman praying. In fact, so had everyone else in the ward. She was that loud. All I had to do was get the black lady started and she invited Jesus into her heart. Then the person in the next bed announced, *"I want Jesus too."*

Before my visit ended, seven women in that room accepted Jesus as their Savior because they had seen this one hard-hearted girl change before their eyes. I felt I had little to do with it, so great was the Spirit's power. The whole event was His answer to that flash prayer uttered before I went into the room.

In the months that followed I enjoyed great success using the technique the Lord had shown me. Hundreds were led to Christ on the streets, and in jails and hospitals. To be the possessor of something from the Lord that was so powerful was almost more than I could hold. Increasingly my heart was burdened to get the plan into more and more lives.

A unique opportunity developed when a nationally known evangelist came to the Baldwin Park-Covina area with a big tent crusade. Enlisting the support of many churches (including ours) in an all-out campaign, the evangelist began seven days of services that produced 56 decisions for the Lord.

Payson and I volunteered to work in the inquiry room, counseling those who came forward in response to the invitation each night. We were inwardly amused over the way the Lord was using us on the streets, going and coming from the crusade. Using the Encounter-

Method of soul-winning (this is the way we referred to the technique God had given us), we were leading fifteen to twenty people to Christ each night.

By the week's end, Payson and I had handled twice as many people as the evangelist with his well-oiled campaign. The Holy Spirit had His hands full keeping us from being critical of the preacher and smug about our success. The temptation to show the evangelist "a more excellent way," was almost too much for us.

Payson sensed it was getting to me. *"You know,"* he cautioned, *"there's no way to go to the man and tell him he's not doing his job as well as he should. That he'd get better results if he knew what we know. He's a famous man and we're nobodies."*

"I know, Payson. He is God's servant and it's his crusade. Yet there must be some way to let him know what God has given us without offending him."

"Why don't we talk to the Lord about it," replied Payson. *"We don't have anything to lose. It sure would be wonderful to get the plan into the hands of someone who reaches so many with the gospel as he does."*

So we went to the Lord.

The Holy Spirit gave us an idea.

Since we were working in the inquiry room, we asked the evangelist if he would be willing to check on the salvation of each new convert after we had dealt with him. He agreed and even let us make a suggestion as to what he might ask. He then positioned himself in the doorway so that he could shake hands with each one leaving the inquiry room. As he took the convert's hand he would ask..."*Did something happen to you tonight?*"

"*Yes, I became a Christian.*"

"*Congratulations, that's wonderful. But suppose someone were to ask you...'How do you know you are a Christian?' What would you say?*"

"*I'd say because I asked Jesus to come into my heart and be my personal Savior—and HE DID! I know I'm saved because Christ is right here, in my heart!*"

When he reported back to us, the evangelist was obviously impressed. "*How did you fellows manage to get them so clearly settled in their faith so fast? Is there something I need to know?*"

That was the opportunity we'd hoped for. The evangelist graciously consented to remain a few minutes after the people had left, and let us deal with him as though he were unsaved. We took him through the plan. When we had finished, he just sat there silently, shaking his head.

When he finally spoke, we knew the Holy Spirit had used us:

"*You know, I almost feel foolish. I've brought people to the altar and then sort of left them on their own to 'pray through' while I prayed over them. That's the way I learned to do it. I can see now that this is not the way to introduce people to Jesus. After tonight, I'll never forget that soul-winning is an introduction to a living Person.*"

The humility of this sweet servant was remarkable.

Without any pretended pride, he eagerly embraced the technique and made it a part of his own ministry. That was twenty-six years ago. Since then, those drawn to Christ under his preaching (and there have been many) receive a personal introduction to Jesus and are soundly saved.

Payson and I floated away from the big tent that night. The experience convinced both of us that the Holy Spirit was going to use us to help His people. We didn't know how, exactly, but we had seen Him open a big door. That evangelist has been a real friend and booster of our work for Christ ever since.

The soul-winning technique had developed to the point where I felt anyone could use the plan to present Jesus to a non-believer. In fact, our daughter Linda, whom I led to the Lord with this plan, was herself using it around the neighborhood to win other kids to Christ.

Margie's mother, Edith, was a good person. We had just taken for granted that she was a Christian since she attended church occasionally, and seemed so sympathetic to the things of God. Once the Seyrings moved to Baldwin Park to be near us, Margie became troubled and decided to use the plan and check out her mother's salvation.

When Margie got her up to the question about receiving Christ, Mrs. Seyring gasped. *"You know, I've never done that,"* she volunteered. *"I've never done that."*

In the quiet of our home, Margie's mother made that

life-changing decision to receive Christ. It was a good decision. Today at 90, she is still active for Christ, teaching God's Word to a good-sized class in the convalescent hospital where she lives.

A few weeks later, I had the same joy while dealing with Margie's dad. He, too, received the Lord. And his life changed dramatically as well.

Margie's mother and dad not long before Hal died of cancer.

Leading Margie's dad to Christ was in the Lord's timing, for shortly afterwards, it was discovered that Hal had terminal cancer. The dreaded disease spread rapidly through his body. One morning I received an urgent call to the Seyring home.

Margie and I arrived before the ambulance came for her dad. He was weak and could not talk. The pain in his throat made food intolerable. His hair was matted. Beads of perspiration glistened on his forehead. Margie was quietly talking with her mother when I went in to see Hal.

"Do you remember the day you opened your heart to Jesus?" I said, taking his hand. *"If you do, just squeeze my hand."*

He squeezed my hand feebly.

I smiled. *"Isn't it wonderful to have Jesus and know that you're going to be with Him?"* I asked. *"And doesn't He give you perfect peace when you're about to leave this body and be with Him?"*

Once again he squeezed my hand. I sensed it was his last bit of physical strength.

Within moments, the ambulance drivers walked in and Margie's dad was taken from the house. I stood on the porch watching the white coach drive off, red lights flashing. Before the ambulance ever arrived at the hospital, Hal had gone home to be with Jesus.

Her father's death would have affected me very differently had it not been for the soul-winning plan. It would have been awful to stand by and watch him die—

helpless to do anything about his soul. But as it was, God not only let me win him to Jesus weeks earlier, He also let me reassure him of his salvation in his dying moments. I would have never known such joy and satisfaction without that wonderful plan.

As I rejoiced in the Lord's goodness to me, I couldn't help but think of all those who have to say good-bye to loved ones, unsure of their salvation. That led me to speculate as to what could happen to the average church if the pastors equipped the members with a plan like this. It seemed the sky was the limit. I was dazzled at the prospects God might have in mind.

It was enough to make me pause and worship Him. As I did, I sensed the next big step in His plan for me—was just ahead.

CHAPTER NINE

A New Vision— The Power Of Print

News of our soul-winning success spread throughout the community. More and more people were wanting to know about it. Since it wasn't possible to give everyone who asked a personal demonstration, it was clear some other means was needed for sharing the plan with others. But how? Once again I was in the place of needing help from the Lord. He'd have an answer.

Yes, He had an answer all right, but it was the last thing in the world I expected. And Dr. James Jauncey was to play a key role in bringing about that answer. This would be the second time he would be used of the Spirit to exert a powerful influence on my life.

It was Professor Jauncey's custom to set aside the

last Friday of each month for any student who wished to present his views on a particular subject. The catch was, the material to be discussed had to be presented to Dr. Jauncey in writing before it could be delivered orally before the class.

I hated writing. In fact, I ducked every class where writing was involved. Term papers were my nemesis. But now I was stuck. If I wanted to present my views on soul-winning, which I did, I would first have to write out the plan. Reluctantly I applied myself to the task, setting forth the techniques, the dialogue, and the four verses.

"Lovett, you ought to try writing," said Dr. Jauncey after studying my presentation. *"This plan is fantastic. Your style is very different, yet simple and direct. And you seem to come across with a lot of authority. I really think you ought to consider writing for the Lord."*

"But I'm no writer," I protested. *"I hate it."*

"Before you get too rigid in your refusal," he exhorted, *"shouldn't you take it to the Lord and see what He has to say about it? You could be resisting the Holy Spirit, you know."*

Ouch, that was direct enough. He had earned the right to be blunt. After all, he'd taken plenty off of me in the classroom. Besides, if it was the Lord's will to make a writer out of C. S. Lovett, it would take that kind of dynamite. But this first blast didn't do it. C. S. Lovett needed more prodding.

The following Sunday I was speaking on soul-winning in my own church. In the process, I demonstrated the complete plan, showing all the little techniques for bringing a prospect to a clear-cut decision in less than ten minutes. When the service was over, various ones came to me, practically demanding that I give them something that would help them master the steps for themselves.

"Well, I guess I could use the paper I turned into Dr. Jauncey. That wouldn't take too much effort," I thought to myself. So I prepared a syllabus which outlined the plan and showed the steps. We mimeographed several hundred copies. As crude as it was, my people seized the plan and immediately began winning souls. Our little church began to grow by leaps and bounds.

In addition, I was frequently invited to demonstrate the plan at various conferences. Every time I would lead someone to Jesus before an audience, a whisper would go through the crowd...*"Why, I can do that!"* The speaking engagements served to increase the demand for the know-how. With each conference, more and more people began urging me to expand the material beyond the mimeographed version and put it into a book for their churches.

At this point, I would give the excuse that I was too busy attending seminary, pastoring the church and ministering in the jails and hospitals. I didn't see how I could do it. Besides, what did I know about printing? In spite of my resistance, the Lord knew he was going to ease C. S. Lovett into writing—one way or another.

That year, 1952, He brought Warren Belknap and his wife, Elenore, to our church. A dedicated Christian, Warren worked in a color printing plant and had years of experience in the trade. The moment he saw the power of the soul-winning plan, he recognized its potential. As the next key person in God's plan to make a writer out of me, Warren began urging me to get the plan in print.

"Well, I suppose it's a possibility," I replied when he first suggested printing a book. Actually I was trying to put him off politely. He was such a dedicated brother. I didn't want to discourage him.

"I have some contacts who can set the type for us," Warren continued, *"so I know the work will be professionally done. I even have a friend who has volunteered to print the sheets on his company's press after hours. You just write out the copy and I'll see to the printing."*

Ouch, that was another good jab from the Holy Spirit. One which was due to bring matters to a head. *"Uh, well, I'll have to pray about it. I'll let you know next Sunday."*

That evening I discussed Warren's words with Margie. She was thrilled. *"Remember when you didn't want to go to that ministers' conference?"* she reminded. *"I urged you to go, and as a result we both ended up saved? Well, I have the same feeling about Warren's suggestion. I think you should do it."*

That settled it. I threw in the towel and went off to talk to the Lord: *"All I asked You for, Lord Jesus, was a way to share this plan with others. I knew You had an answer, but my becoming a writer was not what I thought You had in mind. You know how I feel about writing. I hate it. I don't know anything about it. But if that's what You really want, with Your help I'll become one."*

At that moment, C. S. Lovett and his Father were of the same mind.

That same night I called Warren and told him of my decision. He said, *"Good, now we're in business for the Lord!"* I had no idea what that statement meant at the time—maybe Warren didn't either—but he was surely speaking prophetically. I doubt if either of us could have guessed what was going to flow from that decision.

Using time I didn't think I had, I rewrote and expanded the material from the mimeographed version. Warren planned to produce eight thousand copies. It seemed like an awful lot of work at the time, but several families from the church volunteered to help. We drove to Highland Park, assembled the books by hand, stitched them together and then trimmed them with a large paper cutter.

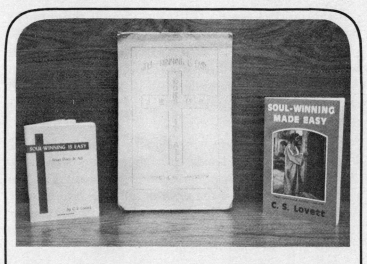

In the middle is one of the original copies of the soul-winning syllabus Margie and I mimeographed in our garage in 1951. A year later I was surprised to find myself rewriting as God brought forth our first book (left). To the right is the 1978 edition, in its 27th year of serving God's people.

By the time the books were done—all eight thousand of them—I was beginning to have second thoughts about the whole thing. They all ended up in my garage. One afternoon I walked out there to look at them. Box after box after box was lined against the wall. There wasn't room for the car.

My spirit was troubled. I hadn't been too wild about the idea in the first place. And all that work. I wondered if we were really on the right track. What was I to do now? I had no outlet for the books. I didn't know eight thousand people. How would I go about distributing them? If I stood on a street corner, I doubt if I could even give that many away.

Deep inside I sensed that every one of those books belonged in the hands of God's people. I knew the power of the plan and what happened in lives where it went. The Holy Spirit knew the people who needed it. So I knelt down beside the boxes, laying my hands on them:

"Lord Jesus, I confess the anxiety I feel right now," I said, running my hands over the coarse cardboard. *"I'm thrilled with the plan You've given us, but I've gone along blindly on the printing of these books. Now we've got boxes of them, Lord, and I don't know what to do with them. If we're in Your will, You're going to have to show us what to do next."*

Suddenly it struck me what we might do. I continued praying. *"Lord, there are two ways we can go with these books. We can either give them away or sell them. But if we give them away, we won't have any money to pay for them, neither will we be able to produce any more.*

"On the other hand, Father, I'm reluctant to get into an offering ministry. I've seen enough of that. I'm just going to believe You want us to sell them for something like, say a dollar, and if You don't object somehow, that's what we'll do."

The Lord's presence was so near. I could almost hear Him saying, *"Go to it, son. Do whatever is in your heart, and I'll work with you. I know your motive is right. So go to it."*

Later, I told Payson and a few others about my conversation with the Lord. We priced the book for a dollar and boldly inserted an ad in one or two Christian magazines—and waited. It was up to the Holy Spirit now.

Then it happened! The Spirit blessed the ads and orders began coming in. As the books went out, people began to win souls to Christ. Even pastors led their first souls to Jesus. We received glowing letters describing their experiences. Hundreds were being won. People told their friends about the plan. In turn, the friends ordered and the results began to snowball. Our supply of eight thousand books was quickly exhausted. We had to place another order.

I was struck with a tremendous realization—we were doing more for Christ with this one book than I was doing preaching. I had discovered the power of print!

The skill the Holy Spirit had given made the Baldwin Park Baptist Church a soul-winning church. I didn't have to give an invitation. Strangers, walking in the front door, were warmly greeted and asked about their salvation experience. Everybody in the church was trained in winning souls. We had no unsaved in our Sunday school. People were continually won outside the church and brought in.

An unsettled feeling was beginning to stir inside me as results were reported with the book. So much was happening wherever it went, that I wondered about the call on my life. Was I really where God wanted me? I knew He wanted me to be a writer, and if one book could increase my effectiveness for Him that much, what would happen if I wrote another?

Yet I had never thought about serving the Lord full time in any capacity other than that of a preacher. To my mind, going into the ministry meant standing behind a pulpit. That's why I was in seminary. Yet here I was, discovering I could reach thousands of people with my pen, but only a few hundred with my mouth. That was bound to generate conflict, one that was to surface in the days ahead.

I had been asked to present the soul-winning plan to a large Baptist church in Whittier, California. The seminar was successful and well attended. The final day, a man walked up and introduced himself as the business manager for evangelist Billy Graham.

"Our association appreciates the thrust you're making and the power of this plan," he said, *"But I wonder if I might ask you a straight-forward question."*

"Sure, go ahead."

"What kind of a program do you have for these people once you've led them to the Lord? What exactly is your follow-up on them?"

The man's question bore in on me. I didn't have a program. In fact, I was suffering no little agony over that very thing. I had assembled a list of people I had led to Christ using the one-on-one basis—around three thousand. Every now and then I would go back looking for some of the new babes. It hurt when a number of them hid as they saw me coming. Others didn't seem the least bit excited over being saved. That disturbed me plenty.

"Well, I don't have one," I admitted sadly.

"The only reason I ask," said the man, *"is that Billy Graham agonizes over this problem. The people seem to vaporize. When civilians enter military service they go through 'boot camp.' This gets them ready for life in the service. But when we bring people into the Christian life, which is far more baffling, we leave them on their own to sink or swim. I was hoping you might have an answer."*

That conversation with Billy Graham's manager plunged me into some serious thinking and praying. To me it was clear the Holy Spirit was in charge of my efforts. He had brought me to Christ and given me this tremendous soul-winning plan. Surely He didn't mean to let it drop right there. I took this challenging conversation to mean it was time for me to lean on the Lord for a follow-up plan.

C. S. Lovett and his Heavenly Father were now going into the "people construction" business to build Christians.

As I diligently inquired of the Lord and searched the Scriptures, the Holy Spirit began unfolding a plan for new converts. I called the plan, "Dynamic Truths for the Spirit-filled Life." It was built on the truth of the believer's two natures—carnal and spiritual, and other basic truths new Christians should know.

As I began teaching our baby believers about their two natures, the results were almost magical. They understood much better the miracle that had taken place in them when they were saved. They knew how to work with the Holy Spirit to gain victory over weaknesses. They became stable and secure, thrilled with the changes they could see taking place in themselves.

In the space of six months, I saw whole families revolutionized after they were exposed to these dynamic truths. Before I knew it, I had a second book on my hands! God's perfect follow-up!

We were now in a position to give soul-winners the follow-up tool they needed. Used on a personal basis with weekly contact, pastors could hold classes for new Christians that would literally transform them right before their eyes. Workers using these exciting truths found they had discovered "Jesus' boot camp." It provided a perfect beginning for new babes in Christ.

Jack Kerr was also a student at California Baptist Seminary when we were starting the church in Baldwin Park. As soon as he learned of our work, he came wanting to help. Before long, he was a close personal friend, and one of the first to see the possibilities of the soul-winning plan. Along with Payson and Warren, Jack wanted to be a part of whatever God had in store for me and the books He would produce through me.

Because of his background in business, Jack believed the best way for us to get our books out was by using the principles of direct mail. Actually, though, the four of us knew very little about it. Having no equipment, we spent hours brushing glue on the backs of mailing labels. Beyond that, we spent time in prayer asking God to anoint the hearts of those who received the books—and to show us how to proceed. The more results we saw, the easier it was to give ourselves to prayer. It was gradually dawning on us what could be done with books—bathed in prayer.

We met at Payson's house regularly. One night he came in with a bundle of mail. The four of us sat around happily opening letters. It was so exciting, listening to people describe how they had won souls to Christ.

"I can't get over all this," said Warren, tears glistening in his eyes. *"With so little effort on our part, look what the Holy Spirit has done. I'm holding in my hands people who have really been turned on to the Lord and are out winning others to Christ."*

We all humbly nodded in agreement, aware that we were holding the treasure of God in our hands.

"Listen to this," Jack announced, tenderly smoothing a letter he had pulled from the stack. *"This brother writes from Michigan. He says, 'I read the plan. I tried it. It works. The Lord has allowed me to lead three people to Jesus this week. I praise Him for putting me in touch with you.' "*

"Wow!" I interrupted, *"That's exciting!"*

"You know," Warren reflected, *"it strikes me we're*

143

doing more for Christ with these two books than we're doing with our whole church here in Baldwin Park. We see one or two saved on a Sunday, but look how many are coming to the Lord through these books! I don't see any limit to this!"

Warren's remark stimulated my imagination. *"Brother, you've just given me an idea. What do you think would happen if our whole congregation saw the power of these books and the church committed itself to putting them into the hands of Christians everywhere! Why, thousands would be saved all over the country, maybe even the rest of the world!"*

"Our whole congregation," gasped Payson! *"How would you ever get them to go for it?"*

"That's right," interrupted Jack, *"you know how our people love the excitement of seeing souls come forward each week. And many of them, especially the young ones, are caught up in the fever of a growing church. How could you possibly get them to trade live souls in the pews, for letters that merely tell about people being saved?"*

"I guess I hadn't considered that," I replied. *"For a moment there, I was thinking only what it might mean to the Lord. Imagine—a whole church dedicated to getting out these tools. Talk about a new frontier! Like Warren says, there's no limit to what could be done!"*

Of course we all agreed it was a great idea, but didn't see much hope of it taking place. Nevertheless, I couldn't shake the possibility. Jack sensed it.

"If you really think we should try to get the whole

144

church behind an idea like this," he asked, wanting to keep his own heart open, *"how would we go about it?"*

"I don't know," I said, scratching the back of my neck. I often do this when I'm stuck for an answer. *"But if the Lord's in this, He'll provide a way. If not through our own congregation, then maybe some other way."* My confidence in Him was rising. The idea had come from Him. I was sure of that.

Each of us discovered the Holy Spirit had inspired an idea that wasn't going to go away. We all sensed the power of the tools He had given us, and there just had to be a way to get them into more lives.

Then something unique happened.

I received an invitation to visit with Dr. J. E. Conant, a well-known evangelist and Bible teacher. I had read Dr. Conant's book, "Every Member Evangelism," which fell into my hands in the early days of my seminary training. It inflamed me. God used it to stir me for the cause of *personal* Christianity. I was delighted for a chance to meet him.

At the time, Dr. Conant was retired, living in the Silver Lake district of downtown Los Angeles. A slightly built man, Dr. Conant appeared in frail health although his spirits were high.

"Oh, I'm so glad you could come," he said, ushering me into the living room. *"I just wanted to meet you and let you know how proud I am of you and your soul-winning plan."*

We talked for several hours. He wanted to know how the Holy Spirit had given me the plan, and I actually took him step-by-step through the approach.

"I just wanted to hear it personally from you," he said gratefully as we brought our meeting to a close.

I thought nothing further about my visit with this precious man until a few weeks later when a second call came. He said he must see me *"as soon as possible."*

His health seemed to have changed overnight. His eyes were deep set, and his gray suit hung loosely to his bony frame.

"I'm dying of cancer," Dr. Conant said in a steady, firm voice.

"Ohhh," I moaned softly, thinking of the great loss it would be.

"But there is one thing I must do before my house is in order," he said resolutely.

"Well, if there's anything I can do, Dr. Conant, I'll be happy to," I volunteered, not really knowing what to say in this situation.

"Brother Lovett, I'm burdened for a successor to carry on the program of making Christianity personal," he said, tears now ringing his eyes.

Dr. Conant walked over to my chair and placed his hand on my shoulder. *"Brother Lovett, I pass my mantle on to you."*

By now, tears were streaming down my own face. Elisha must have felt the same way when Elijah placed his mantle upon him. *"I accept this mantle,"* I said, sensing the power of the Holy Spirit in the room. I knelt in the quiet of Dr. Conant's living room as he committed me to the Lord.

It was this great man's last act for Jesus. Within days, he was home with his beloved Master.

In my mind, things were starting to add up. The results with the two books. The unsettled feeling in my spirit. Graduation from seminary with a number of degrees, all awarded Magna Cum Laude—due solely to the Lord's gracious help. And now this scene with Dr. Conant. I couldn't shake the feeling that my Father was ready to make a change.

I barely graduated from junior college because I lacked motivation. But I graduated from seminary with honors because the Lord had fired my spirit with ambition to serve Him.

Margie had always been a counter-balance for me. If my thinking got too big or far off base, she tended to balance me. It gave me a good way to check the Holy Spirit's leading. Time and time again I went to her with my feelings. By now my vision was that of ministering to millions. I saw my parish as every home that could be reached by the U. S. Postal Service. I felt it was time to burst the bonds of Baldwin Park.

"Of course, I'll be with you, honey," she said, pondering my ideas. *"I've sensed for some time a change was coming. But if we leave the church, where will we go? What will you use for a place to meet? How will you get a thing like this started?"*

"Well, dear, my idea is to have a church WITH a literature ministry," I answered. *"I don't see any reason to leave the church. I'd like to continue as we are, only putting our primary emphasis on the literature end of it."*

"But what will you do if a lot of the people don't like the idea and vote against it?" she interjected. *"That's a possibility, you know. I realize you're excited about the idea, but sometimes your ideas are bigger than many can handle."*

But I was confident. *"I don't see how they could vote against me. After all I'm the guy who started the church. I can't see why they wouldn't welcome the idea of reaching out to the whole country. Naw, I'm sure they'll go along with me."*

Margie smiled. *"The only thing I'm sure of is this— you'd better be ready in case they don't."*

Margie and I talked it out as much as we could, and prayed about it for several weeks before I made the announcement in church. That Sunday I called my message, "A New Vision."

"Brethren, I feel called to serve the whole body of Christ, not just a few here in Baldwin Park," I explained. *"If we were to expand our program from that of a purely local operation to a church with a literature ministry, there's no limit to what we could do for the Lord. He's given us some really powerful tools that win and change men. If we were to dedicate ourselves to getting them into the hands of as many Christians as we could reach, we'd end up with a church that was 100 times more effective than it is now."*

The church was packed but strangely quiet. I sensed emotions were high throughout.

"Some churches use the radio a great deal," I continued. *"Others use television. I picture the postal service as a means we can use to reach out across the entire United States. If we had a literature ministry, we could use the mails. It's a very direct method of communication and an efficient way to use the Lord's money."*

A few people seemed to agree. Others sat there apparently unfazed by my vision.

"I'm talking about a church with a vital job for Jesus," I concluded. *"A church with a mission, a church with a vision. I think we have an opportunity to make a contribution to the body of Christ that no other church has. Can we really afford to pass it up?"*

I fully expected the congregation to rise up in enthusiastic support of my suggestion. I had no reason to believe otherwise. While the matter was being discussed and voted upon, Margie and I took a short walk, leaving the Woman's Club building for a while.

"We're sorry," the chairman of the board of deacons said to me after we returned. *"The congregation voted 145 to 144. They're afraid if we expand the operation, we'll lose the intimacy and emphasis we have now. So they want to keep it strictly a local operation. Your proposal has been rejected."*

"One vote," I thought, *"the vision was rejected by one vote!"*

My face undoubtedly flushed several shades of red. I was stunned by the vote. It was hard to accept. After all, many of the members were people I had won to the Lord myself. The rest were all dear friends who had matured under my ministry. I loved them all and was *sure* they'd go along with me. But now the die was cast. I had put the matter in my Father's hands and He had made His will known.

The following Sunday I met with the board of deacons.

A lump rose in my throat as I handed over the keys to the building to the chairman of the board, along with my resignation.

"We love you, pastor," said the chairman, *"and know you have wonderful ideas, but many of the people here are young and love the excitement of a growing church. It's what most of us need and we don't want to change it"*

Funny how I never really accepted that. The Spirit bore witness. They did need their church the way it was. And if I wanted to make a shift, I should go off and do it on my own. But that didn't make the pain any easier.

So Margie and I drove home—wiping our tears as we went. We were leaving some beautiful Christians behind. But the Lord's direction was clear. I was out of that situation and headed for something else. Convinced He was leading, we soon replaced our tears with eager anticipation. Obviously a big step was ahead—*but what would it be?*

CHAPTER TEN

Something New, Exciting And Personal

Bill Zachary was a real estate man I had known for years. He owned a large two-story house in Baldwin Park which he called the "Good Samaritan House." He had planned to use it as a center for rehabilitating derelicts, even going to the expense of adding a fine chapel that would seat a hundred people. He had a secret longing to preach and this was to be his outlet. But somehow his plans for the house never materialized.

In the timing of the Lord, precisely when we needed His direction, Bill telephoned offering me the use of the facilities. My Spirit went into orbit. *"How did you know, Bill? Did someone tell you I had left Baldwin Park Baptist with no place to go?"* I was curious as to how God had arranged for him to call me at that particular time.

"No, no one told me," he said. *"When my plans changed, I just felt led to do it. The Holy Spirit seemed to say, 'Call brother Lovett and see if this building would fit into his program in any way.' "*

I marveled at the speed with which God had moved.

The next thing was to call some ten or fifteen families who felt as strongly about the vision as I did; among them, Payson, Warren, Jack and their families. When they learned of the call from Bill Zachary, they couldn't wait to get together at the "Good Samaritan House" and see what God had provided.

Our first PC board may have been a handful of nobodies, but our joy is obvious as we pose outside the "Good Samaritan House." (Left to right) Andrew Parish, Jack Kerr, Payson Gregory, Warren Belknap and pastor "Sam."

Later that same day we met in the huge living room on the ground floor and I found myself looking into some pretty excited faces, faces of people who loved me and believed God had just given us the "green light"— Andrew Parish, Bob Leber, Claude Greaver, Lou Leavitt, Doris Allen, Ressa Cousins, Viva Howard, Alice Towler, and Margie's mother Edith Seyring. We now had a ministry and a base from which to operate. When God wants to, He can move fast! Wow!

Everyone was curious, naturally, to see what the Lord had given us. We joined hands for a moment to praise Him, then began a tour of the facility that had been turned over to us practically rent free. You should have heard the "oohs" and "aahs" as we poked our heads in first one room, and then another.

When we had seen everything, we gathered for fellowship in the chapel to sample the spirit of the place and discuss how we might proceed. Alice, a lively eighty-year-old who never lacked for words, was the first to speak up, *"Well now that we've taken the giant step,"* she declared, eyes twinkling, *"it will be fun to see how the Lord will lead us."*

"I'll say," reflected Andrew. *"When God gave pastor Lovett the vision of what could be done with a whole church dedicated to getting the books into the hands of Christians, he never dreamed the Holy Spirit meant for him to start a new one just for that purpose."*

Before I could reply, Ressa chimed in. *"Well, one thing is sure, we may not be as big a church as the one we left, but we're all agreed as to what we want to do. Anyway, the Lord can add to our number as He sees fit."*

"What I'd like to know," asked Payson, *"is how we're going to function. Will we have the same type of program we had at Baldwin Park Baptist?"*

"Sure," I shot back. *"I'll preach every Sunday as always and we'll have Sunday school and prayer meetings. The only difference is, our ministry will be to the whole body of Christ rather than a local operation. Just as some churches use radio and TV to reach out, we'll minister through the U. S. Postal system. It will be the same as before, only our emphasis will be different."*

Jack cleared his throat. *"We've got to remain a local church,"* he said, *"otherwise we won't have a way to develop and test our tools. If we make our materials work in a local church situation, then we know they'll be useful to a big part of the body of Christ."*

"Yeah, and besides that," Warren offered, *"regular church meetings provide the close fellowship we all need. No matter how far our ministry reaches, we must have the spiritual atmosphere of a local body of believers if we're to grow in the Lord, ourselves."*

The handful of people all agreed we should maintain the close fellowship of a local church, but at the same time, concentrate on getting our literature out to the rest of the believers. We viewed ourselves as a church with a special assignment from the Lord—*ministering know-how tools to the whole body of Christ.*

Something was bothering Payson. *"Now that we've decided to expand our ministry to include the whole family in Christ, what are we going to call ourselves?"* he asked bluntly. *"We can't go on as a Baptist church, can we?"*

As much as we all enjoyed being Baptists, we realized it was time to shed our denominational label and think of ourselves as part of the one body in Christ. We therefore needed a new name.

"As you all know, there's a burning in my heart to draw people close to the Lord so they can enjoy Him intimately," I said intently. *"I want everyone we can reach to taste the real thrill of the Christian life—moving in the power of God. My overriding passion is to make Christianity as personal as possible and I wish we could communicate that somehow in our name."*

"Well then, why not just call it Personal Christianity?" suggested Margie.

"Personal Christianity," I repeated, *"Ummmmmh, that feels good. It doesn't communicate the church idea, but it certainly transmits what I feel. What would you think if we called it Personal Christianity Chapel?"*

Everybody seemed to sense what I was saying—Personal Christianity Chapel was a fitting name for our new ministry.

I knew from experience the thrill of having God in my heart; sharing every thought, every feeling, every moment with me, His child. He was, after all, my personal Father. By faith, I could put my arms around Him and embrace Him. In the Spirit, we had great times together—laughing, crying, planning.

I was determined to make this intimate, personal aspect the core of every book, every tract, every piece of literature we produced. I could feel the Lord's eagerness in my spirit, yearning to seize every single one of

His children and hug them all tenderly. I wanted to do it for Him—through our literature. I reveled in my calling to make Christianity as *personal* as possible.

We liked the spirit of the place as we gathered for that very first meeting in the little chapel.

During the week I worked on various writing projects and each Sunday afternoon we held church in the "Good Samaritan House." The worship service was followed by a work session. In that way, the Word of God stirred our hearts and we presented the Lord with an offering of our hands. It was a program of "worship and work."

We used every room in the two-story building. Upstairs people stuffed envelopes with flyers on our books while others addressed and sorted the letters. It was a beehive of activity. As more and more churches and pastors discovered our materials, the mailing list started to grow.

157

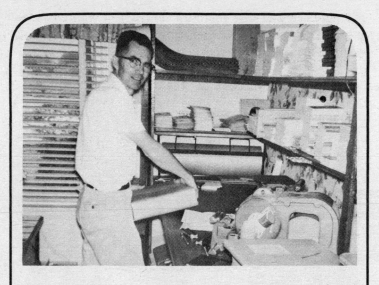

Here are two sacrifices on which the ministry was built: Payson wrapping packages in his bedroom dedicated to Jesus (above); our board examining the new press in Warren's living room (below).

Growth also meant more work for everybody, and in some cases it called for sacrifice. That same year was also the year Payson's wife died of polio. In spite of the sorrow over his wife and the burden of caring for two small children, Payson remained faithful to me and the ministry.

Since he had finished seminary, Payson got a job going door-to-door selling brushes. He barely eked out an existence, but to him it was another mission field. Selling brushes was just a point of contact. Everywhere he went he told people about Jesus and led many to the Lord.

Yet that faithful brother would come home after a hard day's work, take care of his kids, and then work on PC's book orders which arrived in the daily mail. Because he had to care for his children, Payson's home was our first shipping department. His house was filled with stacks of boxes, wrapping materials, trays and mailing cartons. There was hardly a time when he didn't work past midnight. Since none of us drew salaries, it was all done out of love for the Lord and a burning desire to help His people.

As the ministry continued to grow, so did our needs—especially for equipment. Because of his experience with printing, Warren naturally handled that end of the ministry. When we just had to buy a small printing press, Warren took some money that he had been saving for a new car and gave it to us for our first press. He continued to drive his old Chevy, trusting the Lord to keep it going.

Warren remained at his daytime job, just like Payson. But at night, he would do our printing in his garage.

When the nights finally got too cold for him, his wife Elenore, agreed to bring the press into their living room. Whenever Margie and I would go to their home for dinner, we would see the press directly across from the dining room table.

Later we desperately needed storage space for our books. Ressa, a widow in the congregation, owned a house in Baldwin Park which she rented. Instead of renting the house, she allowed us to fill the rooms with our books.

Again and again, needs would appear only to be met by people within our ministry. It seemed to be the Lord's plan for our work to rise on the sacrifices of my people. I was deeply touched by the dedication of people such as Payson, Warren and Elenore, Jack, and Ressa.

The book, "Soul-Winning Made Easy," was highly popular among pastors. Churches bought them in the hundreds as classes were begun to teach the plan. Bible schools and colleges from various denominations also used the book. We found we not only needed a follow-up plan, but we had to develop teacher's manuals as well.

The Lord was ever sending people into my life to help and encourage the ministry. Dewey Lockman, a wealthy citrus grower, was one such person. I met him at a regional conference of the Gideons at Forest Home where I was teaching the soul-winning plan.

A historic meeting of the Lockman Foundation and the Zondervan Publishing House just prior to the release of the "Amplified Bible." In the center is Dewey Lockman (above). A scene taken when I was on assignment in Mexico City, working with translators on the Spanish edition of the "Amplified New Testament" (below).

Years before, Dewey had established the Lockman Foundation, wanting to use his sizeable assets for the Lord. He also owned the Foundation Press, a print shop in Santa Ana, California. Many times he set type for PC books, printing some of the materials on visitation, surveys and teacher's materials.

I was later asked to serve on the Board of Directors of the Lockman Foundation. This gave me a unique opportunity to serve as an editor of the "Amplified New Testament" and participate in the various Bible projects of the Foundation.

Time passed with the momentum continuing. The Holy Spirit was bringing forth a stream of materials from my pen by this time and many of the books were being reprinted with increasing frequency. In conjunction with the writing, I had begun holding soul-winning seminars and conferences throughout the country.

Payson and I had lots of fun presenting the soul-winning plan to churches and conventions around the country.

In doing the seminars, I had the privilege of working with people such as cowboy star Redd Harper who did the "Oil Town, U. S. A." movie with Billy Graham, and Dr. C. M. Ward of the Assemblies of God "Revivaltime" radio broadcast.

It also opened the doors to the Hollywood Christian Group where people like Roy Rogers and Dale Evans, and Stuart and Suzy Hamblen had a great burden for the people of the movie industry.

Once while I was speaking to the Hollywood group, a voice suddenly boomed out from the back of the hall, *"I'm not sure I agree with Dr. Lovett! There are always two sides to every question!"*

The voice belonged to actor David Brian, star of the then-popular television series "Mr. District Attorney." Naturally all heads turned to the back of the room to hear his objection.

I could see David had a point. I didn't agree with him, but his objection had some validity. How was I going to handle it? Show business personalities are very sensitive and a wrong word or the wrong inflection could ruffle feathers. *"Lord, I need wisdom fast!"* was my whispered prayer.

"Well, you can't fight city hall," I quipped, deferring to the distinguished actor. *"I'm not about to take on the District Attorney."*

The audience roared. So did David Brian. The moment had been saved. The Holy Spirit had rescued old CS from a potentially embarrassing situation.

C. M. Ward (Revivaltime) and I had fun posing for this picture, as we ministered together at a conference of California business men (top left). Dr. McGee kindly introduced me to the receptive audience of the Church of the Open Door as we held a great soul-winning seminar (top right). Cowboy star Redd Harper was a real encouragement to me in those days (below).

Dr. J. Vernon McGee, then pastor of the huge Church of the Open Door in downtown Los Angeles, invited me to hold a seminar. Using cutout figures and various props, I dramatized the soul-winning techniques. The participants then broke up into groups, scattering throughout the buildings and I worked with them in individual lab sessions. It was the largest number of people I had ever trained at one time.

Afterwards, Dr. McGee wrote to me, *"This is the most effective thing for bringing souls to Christ that has ever been presented in my church."*

The success in seminars and the popularity of the books created a problem for me. I was constantly seeing and hearing my name everywhere. It was on the books and my picture was in all the advertising. As the work grew, so did the publicity.

In the early days, I didn't think anything of it. But with the literature gushing forth in a paper stream all over the nation, the problem surfaced in my spirit. It was a painful one, for I knew the Lord had not called me to exalt C. S. Lovett. My job was clearly to exalt Jesus. There were nights when I wrestled with the matter until the wee hours of the morning.

Every now and then people would write letters suggesting, *"You need to hide yourself behind the cross, Lovett."* Or, *"If you really want to be used of God, you'll take your name off of everything and make your work anonymous."* It hurt to have people think I was interested in self-exaltation.

The pain intensified when pastor Prentice phoned one day. *"CS, I'm on your mailing list,"* he said, *"and it seems like I'm seeing your name out in front more and more. People are starting to quote you now. So I feel the Holy Spirit would have me caution you against the pride trap. Don't let all that heady stuff give you big-shot-itis."*

I hung up the phone a little shaken. Especially by his closing words, *"Better men than you have fallen into the pride trap."* I'd heard of personalities believing their own advertising and fancying themselves as big shots because of it. Now my old pastor was warning me of "big-shot-itis." Wow! If I felt twinges of pain before, I ached now.

In my heart I knew that all I was, God had made me; and that everything that came from my pen, the Holy Spirit had given me. I had nothing in which I could boast. But now I was burdened—*"Was I embarrassing my Heavenly Father by letting my name go on the books and advertising?"*

Troubled, I went to our PC board—Marjorie, Payson, Jack and Warren. I could always depend on them to be straightforward with me. They knew and felt the call was as much theirs as mine. It had always been that way. If I got out of line, they wouldn't hesitate to check me.

"Are we off base using my name as we do?" I asked sincerely. *"You know how I feel about our stewardship of the glory of God. But with the feedback I've been getting lately, I'm wondering if we're on the wrong track?"*

Always one to see the practical side, Jack shook his head. *"No, I don't think you're out of line at all,"* he said flatly. *"I think we have to use a man's name. People*

166

need a leader. There is no way to follow ideas. God's method is men. I know how sensitive you are about this, but I think you're dead wrong if you feel guilty about it."

"*Besides that,*" Warren commented, "*the apostle Paul had the same problem. At the beginning of all of his letters, he says I, Paul, an apostle of the Lord Jesus Christ. He states his credentials again and again in the Scriptures.*"

"*Not only that,*" returned Jack, "*but Paul exhorts people to follow him as he follows Jesus, and that's simply what you're doing.*"

"*How can you be a leader unless you're out in front?*" Margie asked. Heads nodded around the table. "*You can't lead people from behind,*" she continued. "*David had the same feelings as you do, but God put him right out in front.*"

"*CS, you're just going to have to face the cold hard fact,*" Jack said. "*If you're going to do the job God wants you to do, your name has to be prominently displayed. There's no other way to lead. The only thing you have to be concerned about is that you walk humbly before God and that your motive is pure.*"

"*Jack's right, honey,*" Margie affirmed. "*As long as your motive is right, you can expect God to bless what you do. And those who are disturbed by it will have to take it up with the Holy Spirit. It's their problem, dear, not yours.*"

Tension eased within me. With such agreement by the board, I felt relieved for the first time in weeks. "*I know*

167

you're right, all of you," I said, trying to sum up my feelings. *"I sense God's witness in my heart now. By faith, I'm going to realize my name is just a tool the Holy Spirit is using—nothing more."*

When the others had left the board room, I sat there for a long time thinking about the way they had answered me. But more than that, how I was able to listen to their counsel and accept it as from the Lord—even though it was painful at first. The Lord was indeed changing me, moulding me, and now teaching me how to walk the fine line between being put forth as a personality and keeping myself low before God. If, indeed I was learning to do this, how long would it be before He would test me on it?

The test came a few weeks later when I was speaking before a large convention of a particular denomination. Delegates had gathered from all over the world. My subject was, "How to have no unsaved in your Sunday school." I was outlining some of the steps when a hand was raised off to the left side of the auditorium.

I nodded and a man stood to his feet. He identified himself as a postal carrier by occupation, and wanted to make a comment on what I had just presented. He had a suggestion which he felt would improve the plan, but it would require a definite change in one of the steps.

"You may be right, my brother," I said softly, *"and I will certainly pray about it. If the Spirit agrees with you, I will use your idea instead of mine and thank God He led you to speak up."*

Before I could move to the next point, the wife of the General Secretary rose from her seat and came to the platform. Her eyes were moist, as she asked to interrupt for just a second. *"You know, friends, I was only half-listening to Dr. Lovett,"* she admitted to the audience, *"even though we all know God has given him some remarkable ideas."*

"But," she continued, *"it wasn't until he said to this dear brother over here, 'You may be right,' that he got my full attention. When a man of Dr. Lovett's caliber and credentials is willing to humble himself before an audience such as this and accept suggestions from those of us far less qualified than he, I'm impressed. I'm ready to listen to a man with that kind of humility. To me it is the mark of Jesus upon his life."*

The crowd stood and applauded.

I could only take it as a tribute to the Holy Spirit. I knew what I was when He found me—nothing. He had taken a strong-willed, selfish man and had brought him to the place where he didn't always have to be right.

Now He had taught me the proper stewardship of my name—let it be used for the sake of the ministry, but at the same time realize that all I am and have done, is not of myself, but entirely of the Holy Spirit. Evidently this had to be learned before God could move me to the next big step in His plan. Would it be a fabulous blessing—or a severe test?

CHAPTER ELEVEN

Dealing With The Devil– Personally

"The place is yours as long as you need it," Bill Zachary said when he handed me the keys to the "Good Samaritan House." Little did we know our little church would outgrow those quarters in a year. The time came almost too quickly when we had to get out and find land on which we could build and expand.

Driving down Pacific Avenue in Baldwin Park one day, Margie noticed a "For Sale" sign in front of a house and garage that was situated in a dandy location. It was just a half-mile off the San Bernardino Freeway and on the main street into Baldwin Park. The real estate people quoted a price of twelve thousand dollars for the property and buildings.

"Not a bad price either," the real estate man commented, *"when you consider that huge lot goes all the way through to the next street."*

"It's a good investment," I agreed, having already sized up the possibilities for that big piece of ground. *"I'll talk it over with the church board and let you know if we're interested."*

Here is the property Margie spotted on Pacific Avenue, in Baldwin Park. It took a lot of faith to see a ministry rising from it. Warren and I felt our faith mounting as we walked over the ground.

Yes, it was a good buy. The only problem was we didn't have twelve thousand dollars. That meant we'd have to go in debt, and I didn't like the idea one bit. Rightly or wrongly, I felt that God's ministry should be run on a cash basis. I didn't want Personal Christianity owing anyone for anything.

Nevertheless our board, consisting of Payson, Warren, Jack, Margie and myself, met to consider buying the property. Jack was the most vigorous in protesting against my stand of being debt free.

"I don't see what's wrong with having a mortgage on a piece of property," he argued. *"Our company exists because most people can't afford to buy a home outright. I can't see that being a church makes any difference."* Jack's words carried weight, for by now he had become an important officer in a huge lending institution.

"Well, it's too convenient to have faith in someone else's money," I replied defensively. *"Besides, when you go on a cash basis, it's a lot easier for the Holy Spirit to guide you. When He wants you to move forward, He supplies. When He wants you to wait on Him, He withholds."*

"We don't dispute that," agreed Payson, *"but when you're getting started, you always need help."* After much prayer and careful weighing of the counsel of my board, I relented on the condition that after the debt was paid off, we wouldn't borrow for anything again. Everyone agreed that from then on, we should save up the money until we had enough to pay for our purchases. That became PC's financial policy—cash.

We bought the little house on the big lot. When we moved into it, we began making changes immediately. Between the garage and the back porch, we built a large patio-room where we could hold our Sunday meetings. One of the bedrooms became an office, another the shipping room. Payson came to work full-time as our first salaried staff member. Personal Christianity now had its own quarters with plenty of room for expansion.

172

Payson finally got his own office at PC (above). The other board members pose outside an entrance to the newly enclosed patio (below).

As the Lord supplied, we would move our walls further and further.

The books sold so rapidly it was a problem keeping up with the demand. Then we located John Boewe, a born-again Christian who owned El Camino Press in La Verne, close to our new headquarters. John had a deep commitment to the Lord and a talent for producing books in volume at a rock-bottom price. Those two things attracted us to him.

John's printing operation was small at first, but as we grew in size, so did he. *"I can't keep up with you guys,"* he told me one day as we stood together surveying his print shop. *"You've got me bustin' out of the walls back here. I've got your books piled everywhere. I'm already running two shifts. The Lord is moving your books out faster than I can print them."*

By the mid-1960's, we had expanded the original facility several times and now the place had taken on the atmosphere of a booming ministry. In some ten year's time, PC had developed into a fairly sophisticated literature distribution operation with all the necessary equipment.

One of the things I particularly enjoyed after preaching a Sunday service, was taking visitors on a tour through the buildings, pointing out what Jesus had done. It was fun to boast in the Lord and openly praise Him for His overwhelming kindness. With only a handful of people, He had established for Himself a very effective ministry.

But then came a tour I hadn't counted on. Two building inspectors from the city of Baldwin Park showed up one day, wanting to make a spot check of our expanded operation. The Lord had arranged their visit, of course.

They walked through the buildings looking high and low. *"We never dreamed anything like this was going on here,"* said one of the inspectors, a short man with a tough-bulldog face, thinning black hair and darting eyes.

The other inspector, a tall, gangly man, who spoke with a New York accent, was even more grim. *"You aren't zoned for this kind of an operation,"* he said flatly, shaking his head. *"Why even the city doesn't have the production you people have. This whole thing will have to be reviewed."*

"That's right," agreed the shorter man. After looking over the stacks of books, he handed me an official looking paper. *"We'll let you know what we decide."*

I was stunned. I couldn't believe what I was hearing. PC had done everything possible to secure approval from the planning commission—even to the point of public hearings. But it seemed like a threat against the ministry just the same. The way they talked, it sounded as if we could be closed down.

The building inspectors' threats came to mind during the rest of the day, but I dismissed them, thinking, *"Awh, it's got to be a mistake."*

But at bedtime it was a different story. The scene passed through my mind again and again in endless repetition. Everything they said was rehearsed in my imagination. All the hazards and possibilities. My mind wouldn't let go of it. I tossed and turned like a wild man.

Before long I was saying to myself, *"This is no way for a Christian to carry on. Do what you've told others so often...'commit it to the Lord and forget it.' "* Acting on my own advice, I got out of bed and onto my knees. As sincerely as I knew how, I turned the problem over to the Lord:

"Lord Jesus, there isn't one thing I can do about this. It's Your ministry. You are in complete control of all that happens to it. So I am putting this problem in Your hands. I'm trusting You to take care of it."

Then I got back into bed. Bang—the whole process started in again. Why it was just like the carriage return on a typewriter when you type a line, push the button and the carriage flies back so you can start again. I went through the whole scene, committed it to the Lord, and then started worrying again.

The threat really wasn't all that serious. There was no reason to lie awake fussing about it. I knew by faith the Master had His own solution. Even so, the worry process continued for hours. It was getting more unreasonable by the minute. Then it hit me...

"Wait a minute! Someone else has to be in on this! I wonder if I'm being acted upon by an outside force? This is way beyond anything I would normally do!"

That did it. The Holy Spirit moved within me.

"Jesus wouldn't be doing this to me," I reasoned. *"It must be Satan! Of course, why didn't I see it sooner!*

176

Oh man—if that's the case, what am I going to do about it?"

Praying hadn't helped. My honest commitment to Christ didn't deliver me from worry. Faith in Jesus didn't solve the problem.

Then...from deep within my spirit...the Word of God rose like a surfacing submarine...

"RESIST THE DEVIL AND HE WILL FLEE FROM YOU!"

The Holy Spirit was prodding me to action—against Satan. Wow! I'd been resisting temptation for years, but resisting the tempter himself was a new idea. I gulped. When I considered that he was the "god of this world," goose pimples appeared. There was no way out. The Holy Spirit wanted me to act.

But direct, overt action against the devil scared me. Now Satan's presence became increasingly real. Sweat broke out on my hands. I thought I could feel his ugly breath.

"Lord Jesus," I said rather cowardly, *"don't You think You're the One to deal with him?"* I'd heard people tell of asking Jesus to answer Satan's knock. But the Lord's reply made me realize those were nothing more than cute stories...

"I've already dealt with Satan. Now it's your turn. But don't worry, he's a defeated enemy. He will flee if you resist him in My name!"

Of course I didn't hear those words in actual speech. They rose from deep inside me, where His Spirit bears witness with my spirit. But the message came through loud and clear. The ball was in my hands. It was time to do something with it. But what, exactly?

My mind raced to the wilderness scene where our Lord Jesus was tested of the devil. HE TALKED TO HIM. He said, *"Get thee hence!"* In our day that means —*"beat it!"* Then He followed with a quote from God's Word.

I didn't see how I could go wrong following the example of the Lord Jesus. *"Okay Lord, I'll try."*

Margie had been asleep for hours, so she didn't hear me. I let the words out...

> *"Satan! In the name of the Lord Jesus, GO AWAY! For it is written: 'be anxious for nothing; but in everything give thanks, for this is the will of God...'"*

Then I covered my head. I was sure the ceiling would fall in. I expected *something* to happen. When nothing did, I relaxed. I thanked the Lord:

> *"I did it, Lord Jesus. I resisted the devil in Your name and he fled, just like You said."*

The pressure to worry was gone. I fell asleep.

The next morning I awoke refreshed. Something glorious had happened. I had tasted the thrill of putting Satan to flight! What an experience! I sat on the edge of my bed, drunk with power. Yet it was humbling to realize it wasn't my name Satan feared, but that of our precious Lord Jesus! Oh, that wonderful name! A new respect for the authority of Jesus' name swept over me.

I looked up at the ceiling. It hadn't even slightly cracked, let alone fallen down on me. *"I knew You were powerful,"* I said to Jesus, *"but I never dreamed I would taste Your power in such a mighty way!"*

Without doubt, I had discovered a fabulous secret of the Christian life. It was akin to my first soul-winning experience. I thought back to the first time a person said *"yes,"* to Jesus as a result of my work. It was enough. I was hooked. That first thrill was habit forming, and I wanted more. Now another joy had occurred— equally as thrilling.

I was in no hurry to get up. I lingered on the side of the bed, now bathed in the rays of the sun. But I was basking in the glow of my victory. This was a moment almost as big as salvation.

Victory in the Christian life is something we all yearn for, and now I had the key. The Lord was in it. The timing, the circumstances—everything was just right for me to learn how to deal with the devil. No longer was he just a character in the Bible—he was my PERSONAL ENEMY.

I told Margie of my victory. For the next few days we both had fun catching Satan in the act. We actually found ourselves eager for his next attack, so we could put him to flight. The excitement of working with Jesus' power was almost more than we could stand.

After several weeks of victory, I went to my Heavenly Father.

"Father, I can't believe You've given me this tremendous insight for my life alone. It's too big. Is this some-

thing You mean for me to share with others?"

The more I prayed about it, the more clear it became —I had to write a book on the devil—a book that would get this truth to the whole body of Christ.*

Now you don't just sit down and start writing a book on Satan without some opposition. I knew if I were the devil and someone was all set to write a book on me, exposing my methods and showing Christians how to make me flee, I'd do everything I could to stop him. I'd attack!

Since I knew how to deal with Satan, I could parry those attacks aimed at me personally. But the moment I started banging on my typewriter, he found an ideal target in my daughter Linda. If you want to upset a father, hurt his daughter. Linda had always been such a spiritual girl, even leading others to Christ. But fierce rebellion began to rise in her heart during her teen years and later manifested itself openly when I began working on the manuscript.

Linda has an amazing art talent and I envisioned her using it for the Lord. She was working as a full-time

---

*Incidentally, the City Clerk called asking me to forget about the inspectors' visit. Some paperwork had gotten mixed in the planning office. Now everything was straightened out. Accident? I should say not. The Holy Spirit obviously arranged the experience as a teaching device. He does things like that, doesn't He, just to teach us the stupidity of worry.

assistant in the city library, an ideal place for an artist to display her works. Since her paintings were beginning to sell, Satan easily shifted her eyes from serving the Lord to the money and recognition that could come her way.

Margie and I were crushed. We saw it for what it was—an attack of the devil—but that didn't make the pain any less. It drove us to our knees.

"Precious Lord," I prayed clutching Margie's hand as we knelt together, *"You've given us this wonderful daughter and now she's being deceived by Satan. We know where that road leads. Grant us the wisdom to help her. You've taught us about Satan, now show us how to use that knowledge to deliver our daughter."*

The Lord was quick to answer, and I wasn't off my knees before I knew what to do.

As soon as Linda came home from work, I asked her to step into my study. *"Honey,"* I said, nervously wiping my sweaty palms on my trousers, *"are you still determined to pursue a secular art career?"* I remembered how a few words from my mother had turned my life around and was hoping for a similar miracle.

"Of course, dad," she said firmly. *"I don't see any reason to change my plans. Why do you ask?"*

"Linda dear, I feel that using your talent to make money and gain a worldly reputation is of the devil—especially when you neglect the things of the Lord to do it. As your father, I must warn you that it is dangerous to resist the Lord. If you ignore my warning, He will deal with you as He did with me when I was younger."

I sensed her mounting resentment. *"Dad, I'm 21 years old and I have a right to do with my life as I please. If you and mother want to serve the Lord, fine, but don't expect me to get all excited about the ministry just because you are."*

That hurt. I tried not to show it. *"If you find the going rough as the Lord turns you over to Satan for a good bounce, just remember I'm always ready to help you resist him."* As she left the room, I committed her to the Lord to deal with her in His own way.

That night when Linda went into her room and closed the door, Margie and I prayed desperately. Linda was a stubborn girl. We didn't know what it would take to get to her. Though we had no assurance of the outcome, we knew the Lord had led in warning her. There was nothing to do but wait—and pray. Boy, did we pray.

About midnight moans could be heard coming from Linda's room. As we listened, they got louder and louder. A little later her door opened and we heard her steps as she came into our bedroom. *"Dad,"* she cried, *"I'm under great oppression. I'm going out of my mind. I think it's the devil. Will you pray with me and show me how to resist him?"*

I explained the plan as the Holy Spirit had given it to me. Then, taking her hands, both Margie and I prayed the Lord would give her the strength to use it.

She went back to her bedroom. The moaning stopped. *"Lord,"* I whispered, *"does that silence mean victory?"*

The next morning when Linda came to the breakfast table, her face told us what happened. Margie and I didn't have to hold our breath any longer.

"Dad, mom," she was all smiles, *"I want to tell you what happened last night. I told Satan to go, just as you said—AND HE DID! The oppression stopped and I had the sensation of a huge weight being lifted off me. I guess it took something that strong for the Lord to get through to me."*

She paused while Margie left the table to get the tissue box. I brushed my eyes with the back of my hands. A weight was rising from us too.

"Then," she continued, *"I asked the Lord if He wanted to say anything to me...and you know...as clear as anything, He said, 'Linda there are only two ways to go. Either you're going to serve Me or you're going to live for yourself and the devil.' I decided I wanted to serve the Lord."*

You could see the joy welling up inside her as she related the outcome.

"You were right, dad. Those worldly ambitions were from Satan. And I realized it the split-second he fled. So I have made a decision which I know will please you. I want to work with you and mom in Personal Christianity. I'm going to give notice at the library and quit my job with the city."

Margie and I were filled with praise to the Lord. Not only did He deliver our daughter from satanic deception, but He put His seal on the anti-satan plan. I could hardly wait to get to the typewriter. Urged by the Holy Spirit, I was filled with a strong desire to finish the task and get this powerful tool into the hands of God's people.

Neighbor children pose in front of our newly completed chapel (top). It was fun to minister from my own pulpit. Behind me you can see Linda's 16-foot mural of the "Sermon on the Mount." Her paintings in the chapel add to the spiritual tone of our fellowship (bottom).

As soon as we mailed out announcements on "Dealing With the Devil" the impact was immediate—we had to reorder our supply of ten thousand copies in two weeks. The reception was so overwhelming we had problems keeping the orders filled. In fact, the book was so successful, it provided enough money to build the lovely PC chapel.

Testimonies by the pound began pouring in from those who had learned to deal with the enemy. People wrote of being delivered from the occult, depression, fear and worry. Others were freed from years of addiction to drugs, cigarettes and alcohol. Parents, especially, were grateful for being able to equip their youngsters to withstand the evil pressures of our day.

Letters joyously proclaimed, *"It works! It works! I had no idea I could speak to the devil and make him go away."*

"Next to the Bible, this is the book I treasure most," was the most often repeated comment.

But since "Dealing With the Devil" exposed Satan to God's people, the evil prince himself reacted—creating plenty of conflict. The opposition took many forms. Some people resented the fact that I spoke of Satan as someone who was alive and had a personal interest in every Christian. They naturally didn't believe in a personal devil. A few even suggested I was unscriptural.

Besides the opposing letters, hindrances in the printing of the book occurred. Skids of books burned or were flooded out. One railroad car of paper designated for the book was lost and never found. Even the presses and book binding equipment would misbehave. Our born-again printer cringed every time he saw us coming with another order for "Dealing With the Devil." *"Unexplainable things happen when we're working on that book,"* John complained, *"but give it to me anyway and we'll see what he tries this time."*

Many people wrote saying they had trouble reading the book, even though they wanted its help. All sorts of interruptions would occur whenever they picked up the book. It reached the place where we decided to post a warning in front of the book alerting readers to the fact that Satan would try all sorts of ways to keep them from reading it.

But there was even bigger opposition from several well-known Christian leaders. They criticized me openly. I was refused advertising space in one evangelical publication. *"You're giving too much publicity to the devil,"* the editor said. *"People should forget the devil and keep Jesus in the spotlight."*

A few people even used Scripture verses when they wrote. "Give no place to the devil" (Ephesians 4:27) was one. Somehow they thought exposing Satan made me guilty of giving him too much attention—even though he is the believer's worst enemy.

At first, I reacted against such letters, occasionally writing back defending my stand and accusing the senders of spiritual blindness. I didn't see how anyone could oppose a truth so clearly set forth in the Word. I guess it was a normal reaction, but I failed to see that Satan was merely using those letters to prod me into retaliation.

C. S. Lovett needed to learn how to handle criticism, and his Father had a perfect lesson in store for him.

Hugh Harris, a dear friend whom I had met in seminary, was in charge of the Navigators work in Japan. Aware of my position as a director of the Lockman Foundation, he wrote suggesting we consider doing an update of the 1901 edition of the "American Standard Version" of the Bible. I liked the idea and went to Mr. Lockman with it.

"Dewey," I said, holding out the letter to him, *"this is from Hugh Harris, a missionary friend in Japan. He has an idea I think is right down our alley."* Then I explained how the copyright had run out on the older version and suggested we use the experience gained from doing the "Amplified New Testament" to put out a "New American Standard Bible."

A man with a passion for God's Word, Dewey warmed to the idea immediately. He then asked if I knew of a good man who could head up such a project.

"Yes, I know just the man," I volunteered quickly. *"I have a friend at Fuller Seminary by the name of Gleason Archer. He's a top flight scholar, thoroughly skilled in Hebrew and Greek."*

"Fuller Seminary," repeated Dewey, *"Why I know Charles Fuller real well. He's an old rancher himself. Let's go see if he'll loan us Dr. Archer for the project?"*

Three of us piled in a car and drove to Fuller Semin-

187

ary in Pasadena—Dr. Franklin Logsdon, former pastor of historic Moody Church in Chicago, Dewey and myself.

Dr. Charles E. Fuller, the founder of Fuller Seminary and long time pastor of the "Old-Fashioned Revival Hour" radio broadcast, received us heartily. He offered his full cooperation.

At that particular time, Dr. Fuller's efforts at Fuller Seminary were being severely attacked by the president of another well-known Christian university. *"He's sure been roasting you lately,"* brother Logsdon said, commenting on some rather critical remarks which had appeared in several religious periodicals.

A barrel-chested man with a full head of white hair, Dr. Fuller leaned back in his chair and smiled. *"Ye-e-e-e-s-s,"* he responded with his characteristic drawl, *"bless his heart."* That was all he said, but it was so full of love.

When I saw how that giant of a man handled the sharp, biting criticisms which had been leveled against him and his work, I was floored. How unlike him I was. I would never forget that moment. That big man had such a great job to do for Jesus, he wasn't about to get caught up in a battle of words with anyone. And on top of it, he was obeying the Scriptures—returning good for evil (Matthew 5:44)!

In that same moment I knew why I was there! It was exactly what I needed to see—*and do!*

From that time on, I made an agreement with the Lord. Personal Christianity was not my ministry—it was His. I purposed never to defend it publicly. Since it belonged to my Father, He could handle the criticisms.

Thereafter, when letters arrived criticizing me, any of my writings or the ministry, I simply wrote back... *"You may be right! God bless you. C. S. Lovett."* C. S. Lovett had learned his lesson. Never again would it be necessary for him to retaliate against a precious brother or sister in the Lord.

CHAPTER TWELVE

Tested By Fire!

After we had lived in Covina for many years, the Lord did a nice thing. Directly across the street from Personal Christianity, and situated on the corner, was a cozy, three-bedroom home with a large study. It became available and the church bought it as a parsonage.

I sold the house in Covina, and Margie and I moved in. Now we could be close to the ministry and the people we loved most—our PC family. But that wasn't the only change to occur.

Payson Gregory, my beloved co-worker for so long, received a special call of the Lord to work among prison inmates and as a hospital chaplain. After all the years of sacrifice and struggling together, it was hard to see him go. I felt as Paul must have felt when it came time for him to say good-bye to Barnabas.

"You know Sam," Payson's heart was breaking as he embraced me, *"we've been through a lot together. I'd never leave you unless I was sure it was God's will...you know that, don't you?"*

Yes I knew that. I also understood his decision. Payson was a down-to-earth man, not happy unless he could get his hands on souls—directly. PC was getting big now. He had charge of the packaging and shipping department. The larger the ministry became, the further he got from the firing line.

"I won't try to talk you out of it, PG." I knew I couldn't anyway. *"So, we'll say good-bye and know each has a place in the other's heart forever."*

I didn't know what I was going to do without Payson ...but the Lord did. Unknown to me, Warren and Elenore Belknap had been praying about coming to work full-time at PC. The very next Sunday afternoon, Warren approached me.

"You're wondering who's going to fill Payson's shoes, aren't you?" Warren asked timidly. *"Well, I have a suggestion. Elenore and I have been praying about it and we feel the Lord would have me quit my job at the color printing plant and work at PC full-time."*

"Warren!" I exclaimed, *"You'd be leaving a high-paying job!"*

"I know," he replied, *"but we've been arranging our finances and we figure we can get along fine on a smaller*

191

salary from the ministry."

My heart sang with joy. The Lord may have taken Payson from me, but He had Warren ready to fill the gap. Elenore came with him. Together they supervised the office and shipping departments. Elenore got back her living room when we moved our small press into the new pressroom. It was great having such dedicated people in those key spots.

They ran the ship so smoothly, I didn't even need to know what was going on. That left me free for more writing, the thing God wanted me to do. It was blessed having the work in the hands of people who loved me.

The office and shipping departments were in the dedicated hands of Warren and Elenore (at both ends), and their crew of Margie, Linda and Edith.

192

As more years passed and the ministry continued to grow, it became obvious another of the PC board members, Jack Kerr, was going to be needed full-time. A Licensed C.P.A., he had donated his services over the years and had become a close personal friend. In the interim, he had worked his way up the ladder to become the chief accounting officer of a huge lending corporation. To exchange his fat salary in the world for the meager one of a Christian ministry, would be a great sacrifice.

But God had been working in his heart too. Unknown to the rest of us, Jack had also been getting his financial house in order. If I had known that, it would have been easier to approach him about coming to work at PC full-time. As it was, I felt a little shy.

"Jack," I said probing cautiously, *"you work with our books and know our accounting needs better than anyone else. In your opinion, how close are we to needing a full-time accounting department?"*

He knew where I was heading and was way ahead of me. *"I think we're ready now,"* he offered. *"In fact, I think I've got things worked out in my own program so that I could come to work full-time in about sixty days."*

I didn't say anything for a second. I couldn't. Your heart melts when people believe in you and back their confidence with sacrifices like that.

Jack is an orderly man. He said sixty days. Exactly

sixty days later he joined the PC staff. Then we had another department run by someone who loved me. As a result, I no longer had to give a single thought to the financial end of our ministry. It was a glorious feeling to know the money people sent in would be in competent hands.

Another responsibility was lifted from my shoulders when the Lord made it possible for Jack to join our full-time staff.

Through the years, it was fun having the different families come on staff and work full-time for Jesus. For most, it was the fulfillment of a dream. Andrew Parish came with his dear wife, Tressa. They had been with me from the start, and this was the reward of their faithfulness.

When we outgrew the old press and acquired our two-color Heidelberg we needed a dedicated pressman. So the Lord sent Gene Gardner to us. Gifted with a lively sense of humor, Gene added a lot of spice to our fellowship.

Warren's son, Glenn Belknap, had grown up in the ministry. Close to the age of my daughters, he used to ride stick horses with them around the church when they were kids. He is part of the second generation growing up in the ministry. Glenn received training in the computer field. To him fell the task of directing PC's computer operation. Later he became a board member.

Glenn points with pride at the new computer the Lord gave us. This particular type, with its unlimited capacity, brings our vision within reach.

I rejoice in the fact that God gave me a daughter in Linda. From the time she could hold a pencil, she was drawing. After her decision to serve the Lord, she came to work at PC alongside her father. She became an artist for the Lord and PC's art director.

Linda displays one of the reproductions of her recent "Christ at the Door" painting. To have my daughter in the work with me is truly a blessing.

My younger daughter, Donna, worked in the office for many years. Her wedding in August of 1969 was the first to be held in our new chapel. Several years before, I had the joy of leading her future husband, Randy Hettema, to the Lord.

It was quite a thrill to perform the wedding for my daughter Donna Lee to Randy Hettema (top). More thrills came when Donna and Randy made me the grandfather of Jayme almost four years ago and David this year (bottom).

My wife, Margie, had been at my side from the first day. Opening the letters that people write, became her ministry. She loves the job. *"It keeps me close to the people,"* she says, *"for when I hold those lovely letters in my hands and read the tender things our people say, that makes it PERSONAL Christianity for me."*

Margie is the first person to open the mail. We never get tired of reading letters from the many friends God has given us all across the church.

When all of us gathered on prayer meeting night to lift the week's mail to the Lord, we'd sit in a circle. It seemed more like a family get-together than a prayer meeting. The bond was so close, and getting tighter. What a team. What a fellowship—husbands, wives, children. It all seemed so ideal, so perfect...until...

"Knock...knock...knock." The rap on the door of my study was so faint, I almost didn't hear it.

"Come in," I called.

Warren's head appeared around the doorjamb, *"Can I see you a minute?"*

I looked up from my desk where I had been laboring over a manuscript for several hours. Warren wasn't his normal, cheerful self. His face was ashen, his lips trembled.

"Sure, come in," I answered. *"What is it, brother?"*

Taking a seat opposite me, Warren poured out his heart. *"I've just come from the hospital. Elenore has cancer. The doctors say it's terminal. It's in the lymph glands. They say it has already spread throughout her body. It's the most virulent kind."*

Cancer! I was stunned.

I didn't know exactly what to say. All sorts of things raced through my mind. How could it be? Elenore was such a vital part of the ministry. Not only did she help in the office, she was our church pianist. She and Warren had made so many sacrifices. The ministry was just reaching the place where they could see the harvest of their labors.

199

"Warren, we know God loves Elenore," I said softly, searching for the right words with which to comfort him. *"There's no way for this to come into her life unless God allows it. We'll just have to look on it as a test. I think what we need to decide now is whether we're going to get an 'A' or an 'F.' "*

That seemed to shift his mind to the Lord, providing some relief.

"I've known you all these years," I continued, *"and I've watched you grow. I know how closely you walk with the Lord. You can handle it. In fact, we'll handle it together,"* I said reaching across the desk to clasp his hand. *"All we have to do is keep in mind some of the fabulous things the Lord has taught us about our graduation."*

The next Sunday arrived. Elenore was in her place at the piano. The singing wasn't quite as cheerful as usual during our service. Word had spread quickly and everyone knew she was dying. They all wondered what would be her reaction to the situation.

When it came time for testimonies, Elenore was the first person to her feet. A medium-height, reddish haired woman with bright blue eyes, she was eager to settle the fears she knew to be in the hearts of her friends. There were no outward signs of her sickness except that she moved more slowly than usual.

"I know you're all aware I have cancer," she said candidly, *"and you're probably wondering how I feel. I want each of you to know how fortunate we are to be in a fellowship like PC, where the emphasis is placed on a personal relationship with the Lord. The things I've*

200

learned here have prepared me to face this test with cancer."

The congregation seemed to relax as Elenore spoke of applying what she had learned at PC. It was great to see those truths in action before our eyes.

"You know my hope is not set on anything in this life, not even Warren...but on Jesus. All my treasure is laid up in heaven waiting for me. And my personal relationship with the Lord is carrying me through this situation. At this very moment I can feel His arms around me. I can even hear His voice in my spirit saying everything is under control and right on schedule."

I could hear a few sniffles throughout the audience. *"Praise the Lord,"* someone said. A chorus of *"Amens"* followed.

Elenore continued, *"I want you to know how I feel about dying. I'm not afraid to talk about it, I want to. In my spirit I feel marvelous. If the Lord wants me to go, I'm ready for my graduation to glory. If He wants me to stay, I'm ready for that too. As all of us here at PC know the Lord's way is the only way. I'm at perfect peace about it, because I've learned to keep my eyes on Him."*

There were few dry eyes in the church when she finished. Everyone walked from the service enthused and thoroughly blessed by Elenore's testimony. She was living proof that the truth does set God's people free. Here she was, facing death, yet totally free of any fear. Some asked themselves, could they do the same thing if they were Elenore. I was asking myself how I would react if it were Margie? No glib answer came.

201

Elenore was in and out of the hospital for therapy. Several months passed. And then one day Warren sent for me. Elenore's condition had worsened. She was back in the hospital and asking for me. The doctor's report was very bad.

I was nervous and tense when I arrived at her side. I wanted to cheer her up, but my own heart was heavy. I didn't want to lose her. We all loved her so, and she was such a vital part of PC.

Her hand was cold, almost clammy when I lifted it. She had been asleep but the expression on her face was angelic when she awoke.

Once again I struggled for the words to say. *"Elenore, I..uh...,"* I stammered. She interrupted me. I was grateful she did. I didn't know what to say.

Her words were barely above a whisper. Her strength was fading. *"You don't have to say anything. Jesus and I have been talking about it. I can hardly wait. I love Him so."*

It was hard holding back my tears.

"I want to thank you for introducing me to this relationship with the Lord," she whispered. *"He's so close I can feel Him holding me."*

She squeezed my hand a little tighter. I excused myself for fear of breaking down emotionally. But I walked away from that hospital realizing I'd seen a greater miracle than physical healing. I had seen a Christian face death with joy and a testimony that shouted, *"Jesus is the answer."* Death had been defeated in that room.

The next morning as dawn was breaking. Elenore graduated to the glory awaiting her.

I realized the truths that strengthened Elenore so mightily had to be shared with God's people. The Lord had already made it clear we should gear our books to the needs of His people. Death is something we all have to deal with.

In time, the book, "Death: Graduation to Glory," was finished. The title came from Elenore's own wonderful remark. The terrific response from this book told us that, once again, we had fulfilled a need that existed in the body of Christ. The Lord had used the experience with Elenore to confirm the truths we were teaching about death.

In the years ahead, the Holy Spirit used a variety of ways to move me in writing other need books on divorce, godly wives with unsaved husbands, healing, children, and problems with overweight.

As books were developed in areas where God's people were hurting, the ministry mushroomed. From the very beginning, we committed ourselves to pray for every individual who contacted us by mail. When the volume of mail grew, we felt even more determined to pray for each one by name, even though there were thousands of letters a week. Everyone in the fellowship agreed that our "success" was due to the power of prayer.

The prayer meeting is the "engine" of our ministry. No matter how long it takes, we remain in prayer until everyone who writes to us is individually lifted to the Lord—BY NAME.

Our mail was filled with testimonies proclaiming joy of vile habits broken, busted marriages restored, sick bodies healed, rebellious children reformed, and churches revolutionized. Christians were coming alive everywhere—learning to walk in the power of the Spirit.

Our mailing list reached the one hundred thousand mark, then it went to three hundred thousand. When it reached five hundred thousand, everybody felt it was just a plateau. We hadn't even scratched the surface. There were still millions of Christians to reach. We began working with other dedicated organizations, and as a result, our mailing list zoomed to over three million in five years. It seemed we were on the road to world-wide recognition.

As the years went by, God transformed the little house on Pacific Avenue into the expansive headquarters pictured at center. The chapel can be seen on the far right.

One sunny afternoon, Dr. Frank Hutchinson, my dentist and close Christian brother, and I were flying a single engine Cherokee Warrior about one thousand feet above Baldwin Park. As we flew over PC, I secretly admired the building complex as it spread out before me. I drew a deep sense of satisfaction that it had taken in so much of the surrounding area. It was an imposing sight from the air.

"Wow, CS, look what you've accomplished," a voice whispered, as my eyes surveyed the facilities. *"Look what you've built with your pen. Not many can look down on something so imposing. And to think it's all debt free! You really worked hard to create all this."*

Pride swelled within me. My head nodded instinctively to the suggestions. I liked what I was hearing. The voice seemed to come from inside the plane. I looked in the back seat. No one was there. It didn't come from Frank sitting beside me. He was busy flying the plane.

Then I realized the source—it was Satan's voice! Too bad I didn't recognize it sooner, for my thoughts were interrupted by another voice. I blushed—deep red—when I recognized the second voice. It was the Holy Spirit, and His words jarred me back to reality:

"Remember CS, that day in the shower when you took a good look at yourself? Remember how worthless you felt? That you were no good, just a user of people and had no value whatsoever. Remember asking what good you were to anyone, and you had no answer?

"That day I had My eye on you. I was looking for a man who was absolutely worthless. I needed a worthless

206

man for the job I wanted him to do...and you were My man.

"All that you have become since...and all that you have done since...has not been done by you. It was due to Me and My power working in you. I'm just using you to show forth My glory. You are simply a tool in My hands. So don't forget that day when you were nothing in your own eyes. You're still nothing—apart from Me!"

I looked at the buildings again. They seemed different this time as I pondered the Lord's words. Humbled by the Spirit, I prayed, *"Thank you, Jesus, for taking a proud, stupid, worthless fool like C. S. Lovett, and using him for your glory. I apologize for permitting those boastful thoughts to enter my mind."*

The purring engine droned on. Then Frank banked the plane into a steep turn for another pass on the way back to the airport. I gazed down at PC. I needed to recommit it to my Father:

"Father, all this is Yours, not mine. You built it and You own it. You can do with it whatever You please... even burn it to the ground, if that's Your pleasure. I mean it Lord, it's Yours."

It's easy in the flush of spiritual emotion to say lofty things to the Lord. We all do that, never expecting Him to test what we say. But a commitment such as I had just made can't be counted until it's tested.

Several weeks later, I was in my study, across the street from the church, pecking away at my typewriter, when I heard a commotion outside. There is a row of windows on the street side, but they're high. I can't see out unless I get up from my chair. I don't usually rise unless something special seizes my attention.

At first I didn't pay any attention, but the noise got louder. I paused in my typing to listen for a moment, but then decided to continue. Next I heard sirens. They stopped outside. I wanted to finish a page while the Holy Spirit was feeding me ideas, so I didn't jump right up. Finally I caught the sound of excited voices outside.

"I'd better see what this is all about," I said to myself.

Swinging around in my swivel chair, I rose to go to the windows. To my horror, huge clouds of black smoke were billowing upward from the PC buildings. Orange tongues of fire licked through the dense smoke. My heart sank. The church was on fire! Fire trucks and people were everywhere.

Here was the sight that greeted my eyes when I reached the window. My heart sank. The Lord was taking me up on my commitment!

208

For a moment I faltered. *"We're going to be wiped out,"* was the first thought that entered my mind. But then the Holy Spirit reminded me of the noble commitment I had made a few weeks earlier.

"Wait a minute, CS," I said rebuking myself, *"those buildings belong to your Father. You committed them to Him. You told Him He could burn them down if He wanted to. So you might as well relax and see if you can't get a good grade on this test—just like you tell everybody else to do."*

As it turned out, that's exactly what it was—a test. Workmen patching the roof had overturned a pot of boiling tar and the spreading tar had caught fire by spontaneous combustion. Man, does tar make smoke. There was only minor damage. The roofers had everything back in shape in a couple of days.

Even so, I knew my commitment had been *tested by fire!*

It was clear now, the Lord had C. S. Lovett on a short tether.

He had used a fire to show me how easily He could take my job away, if I should get out of line. Another little tug on the rope would remind me of that day in the shower. From now on it wouldn't take much to make me blush in my spirit and say, *"Forgive me Lord, when I forget I am nothing without You."*

I was finally at my Father's beck and call. But I didn't mind. It meant I would stay in His will. It was now safe for Him to broaden His use of C. S. Lovett.

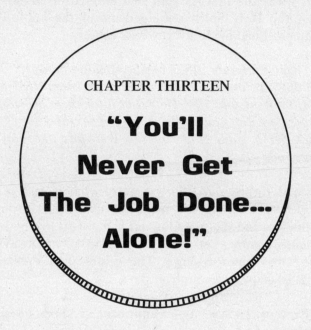

CHAPTER THIRTEEN

"You'll Never Get The Job Done... Alone!"

Millions of books had been sold by late 1976. PC's headquarters on Pacific Avenue had been expanded several more times to accommodate the growth—yet everything was still debt free. We had not deviated from our original policy and the Lord had met every financial need.

The country was caught up in the "born-again" craze. The words "born again" were appearing on the covers of national magazines and America had elected a born-again president. Soon afterwards the Lou Harris poll came out with the results of a survey showing how many in America claimed the born-again experience.

Out of a population estimated at roughly 210 million, the poll reported ten per cent or more claiming to be born again. If the poll was at all accurate, that translated into twenty-one million genuine Christians.

"Twenty-one million!" I thought to myself, as I sat studying the report. *"At least it gives me a clue as to the size of the burden God has laid on me! If there are that many in the U. S., how many must there be in the whole world?"*

The whole world! My mind went to the world situation—the explosive balance in the Mideast, the money crisis, Russia's huge military build-up, the lawlessness, pollution—everything pointed to the fact this was *the last generation!* If so, my burden seemed impossible. Time was too short. I had to talk to my Father about it.

"Heavenly Father," I prayed earnestly, *"You've called me to minister to the whole body of Christ with the books You've given me, and I haven't scratched the surface. Our mailing list of 3.2 million is so tiny by comparison and we're not reaching all of them on a regular basis.*

"Besides, Lord," I continued, *"the millions of books we've distributed so far are but a drop in the bucket compared to the need. At the rate we're going, how can I hope to reach the 21 million in time—let alone serve the whole family? The gap is too big, Father. You've got to help me!"*

Of course my Father had an answer. He wouldn't call me to a job and not have a way to get it done. I knew I could count on Him, but what form would His answer take? From what direction would it come? *"Patience, son,"* He whispered.

Patience was right. The Lord let me wrestle with this problem for some time. I prayed hard, but no answer. It seemed my Father wanted to test my determination. Finally I shared the futility I was feeling with the board and my PC family. As evidence of our sincerity, many of us fasted to make sure the flesh wasn't motivating our prayer request.

Months later my office received an important phone call. A well-known television evangelist was in town and his staff was checking out the possibility of a meeting. They said he wanted to meet me. I had always wanted to meet him. He was a man who had led thousands to Christ and raised millions of dollars for the Lord's work. At first it didn't dawn on me that he might be part of God's answer in some way.

The following afternoon I was met by two of his "advancemen" in the lobby of the Hilton Hotel in Beverly Hills. They cordially greeted me and Jack Kerr, who had accompanied me. The next thing I knew, we were standing outside a door on the fourteenth floor. One of the men knocked lightly.

The door opened and the evangelist's tall figure filled the doorway. *"Come in,"* he said, extending his hand in greeting. *"I'm so glad we could get together. I've followed your ministry for years and I appreciate the fine work you're doing."*

As we filed into the luxurious suite, the smiling evangelist pointed to a chair where I should sit. Jack sat near me. One man stationed himself by the telephone. Two others took places on the sofa. Everything moved so orderly, I could tell our host was on a tight schedule.

Before I could say a word, he set me at ease. *"Brother Lovett,"* he began, *"I've watched your books take hold and your ministry grow, but I've noticed an area where I think you need help. I asked you here today because I believe I can help you if you level with me."*

I never guessed this meeting was to help me. I thought we might be exploring ways to work together. But once he said that, I settled more comfortably in my chair. It would be easier opening up to a man displaying an interest in what I was doing.

"You know," he continued, *"I think I've read all of your books and they've been a real blessing to me. It's obvious the Lord's hand is upon you. But you know— I'm not sure what you're trying to do. How about really leveling with me and lay out for me just what you ARE trying to do?"*

I mulled over his question for a moment, wanting to explain my calling as simply as I could.

"Well," I began, *"let me start off by saying I am called to minister to the body of Christ. From the day I was saved, I knew I was not to be an evangelist, such as you are. But rather I was called to serve the brethren. My burden is for God's people. In fact, I have such a burden for them, I ache inside."*

That remark intrigued him. *"I'd be interested in know-*

213

ing what would give you a burden like that?" he asked, a little puzzled.

"I'm sure you'll agree," I continued, *"that time is short. The Lord's coming can't be far off now. Yet, if you were to ask the average Christian if he is ready to meet the Lord and have his life evaluated, how do you think he'd answer?"*

The evangelist leaned back, stroking his chin thoughtfully. *"Oh, he'd probably tell you he was ready, but not as ready as he'd like to be."*

"Exactly," I was eager to press my point. *"Most of God's people are not as ready as they could be...and they know it! God has called me to HELP THEM GET READY."*

"I think I understand what you're trying to do," he assured me, *"but just how do you propose to get the job done?"*

"We're a ministry of helps," I replied, *"and we bring that help to God's people with books. It has been our experience that books provide the most powerful way to change lives. This is why our Lord chose a Book (the Bible) to preserve and transmit His revelation. The books the Holy Spirit has given us contain the know-how God's people need in order to be ready to stand before the Lord. I expect to fulfill my calling by getting these books into the hands of as many Christians as possible."*

"That's your real burden?" he asked, pinning me down.

"It sure is," I affirmed. *"I don't want any Christian I*

214

can reach to 'shrink away from the Lord in shame,' as the apostle John puts it. And unless they are ready, that's what'll happen."

The evangelist nodded as I spoke. Then his tone became more serious. *"I asked you to level with me. Now I'm going to level with you. I go along with what you're saying. But I can tell you right now, YOU'RE NEVER GOING TO GET THE JOB DONE THE WAY YOU'RE GOING ABOUT IT."*

It was my turn to be puzzled. *"What do you mean?"* I asked, straightening up in my chair. He was talking about the *failure* of my ministry.

"Well, over the years, you've sold your books, making them available to those who could pay for them. I understand you sold them so you could print more, because you believed that was the best way to do the job. But you are wrong in this. You're just not going to get the job done that way."

He was leading up to something vital.

"But isn't that the best way to handle a book ministry?" I querried, thinking of how successful we'd been so far.

"In the business world," he replied, *"I'd say yes. And coming from a business background, such as you have, it's natural for you to think that way. But the Lord's work is different. You can't run a ministry like a business. To do the job you're talking about would take a corporation bigger than General Motors—and God isn't in the corporation business—HE'S IN THE PEOPLE BUSINESS!"*

215

My mouth fell open. This man of God was telling me flat out I *couldn't* succeed. *"You mean I'm on the wrong track?"* I blurted.

The evangelist explained. *"In watching you over the years, I get the feeling your ministry is a private club. You've got your bills paid. And with twenty-five or thirty people, and the help of the mailman, you expect to reach the whole body of Christ BY YOURSELVES! God doesn't work that way. He likes to use people— lots of people!*

"Sitting here and talking with you, I realize you don't feel that way at all. But when you offer your materials only to those who can pay for them and don't share your ambitions or needs with anyone, you give the impression you don't want anyone's help. To me, that smacks of an independent spirit. I think you're secretly proud of the fact that you don't have to go to anyone but God with your needs."

Ouch! That stung! A conflict surged within me. Was he right when he said we might be proud of the fact that we went to God alone for our needs? I was inwardly pleased that we had never asked anyone for a penny, and often boasted about it. But was I right? Was the Holy Spirit raking me over the coals? But my host still had more to say.

The evangelist shifted uneasily in his chair, trying to make it as painless as possible. *"In all the time I've followed your ministry, I don't recall your ever saying to your people, 'I need your help! I need your prayers. I've got a job that is too big to handle alone. If you don't help me, it won't get done!' You see, when you don't share your needs and ambitions with others, you give the impression you don't want help."*

216

I started to protest, but he silenced me with a wave of his hand. He wasn't finished. *"As it is,"* he explained, *"you sell people a few books and that's the end of their involvement with you...no matter how much they like you or your work. You leave them with nothing to do. You don't give them any way to participate in the ministry with you.*

"Besides, it's SELFISH not to let them help you! You don't have to feel like you're begging when you ask God's people for help. This is HIS WAY! His children NEED a ministry to get involved in, as much as you need their help. What's more, there are very few ministries around that really change lives the way yours does. So it's a downright shame to let pride and selfishness keep others from working with you—especially when there's no way to get the job done on your own."

My stomach tightened into a knot. What he was saying contradicted one of my deepest convictions. Twenty-five years earlier when I had prayed over those cartons of my first book, I was convinced the Lord wanted the books to go only to those who could pay for them. That way I could operate His ministry without having to ask anyone for help.

But the Spirit bore witness to the truth of what the evangelist was saying. After all, the Lord had called me to minister to the whole body...yes, I might need help if it was going to get done.

"Suppose we considered such a dramatic change in our ministry," I asked, now more willing to accept his words, *"how would you suggest we go about it?"*

"Tell God's people honestly that YOU NEED THEIR

217

HELP in what you're trying to do. And that YOU CAN'T DO IT ALONE. Then let the Holy Spirit take it from there."

He was at ease with the close of his exhortation. *"The Lord will handle the shift for you. If you decide to open the door, I think you'll find the Holy Spirit has people ready to help you. I know from my own contacts about the country that many Christians believe in you and would welcome a chance to help you get the job done."*

"You could be right," I relented rather meekly. *"We're an organization that preaches change, so I guess we should be willing to change too."*

We'd heard what the Spirit wanted us to hear—and it was plenty. I felt I had all I could take. If this interview was God's answer, would I accept it? I wanted to leave. I got up from my chair.

"You were so gracious, my brother, to invite us and give us the benefit of your counsel," I said, offering my hand. *"You've certainly given me plenty to pray about."*

"I hope you don't think I'm critical of your ministry," he said apologetically, *"because I'm not. I'm thrilled with what you're doing and I want to see it made available to Christians everywhere. What I've told you was something I believed God wanted me to say."**

The evangelist embraced us warmly as Jack and I said good-bye. We left the suite and walked down the hall.

---

*NOTE: When the evangelist learned God had used him to affect a turnabout in our ministry, he asked us not to mention his name. He wanted the Holy Spirit to have full credit. I felt obliged to honor his request, giving my word not to reveal his identity.

The evangelist's words echoed in my mind..."*YOU'LL NEVER GET THE JOB DONE...IT'S SELFISH NOT TO LET OTHERS HELP YOU...CHRISTIANS NEED TO HELP YOU AS MUCH AS YOU NEED THEIR HELP...*"

Somehow I felt the way I did years before after that godly woman pointed her bony finger in my face and proclaimed, "*You're fighting the Lord.*" Her words had proven to be true. "*Could the evangelist's words be the same? Was I fighting the Lord in this matter as well?*" I asked myself.

At the end of the hall a huge picture window looked out over the city of Los Angeles. Jack and I paused for a look. A broad expanse of buildings stretched for miles. Below we could see cars and trucks whizzing along the freeway beside the hotel. The city was alive with activity. It was an unusually clear day for our smog-bound city.

Suddenly I felt the need to talk with my Father... *alone.*

"*Jack, do you mind if I stay here a moment,*" I asked, sensing the call to prayer. "*My Father wants to talk with me.*"

"*Not at all.*" Jack was used to this. "*There's a phone booth back there in the hall. I should check in with my secretary. See you in a bit.*"

The Lord and I enjoyed the view together. It was breathtaking, inspiring. I knew there were Christians out there, many of them caught up in the hustle and bustle of making a living, raising children and running their households. "*If You should come, Lord Jesus, would*

219

You find them busy for themselves or for You? How much time do I have? Is it true I will never get the job done the way I am going about it?"

If we at PC couldn't do the job by ourselves, then there *HAD TO BE A CHANGE* in our approach. More questions poured through my mind. Was my failure to ask the help of others a roadblock to the Holy Spirit? Had God used this renowned evangelist to put His finger on the final barrier that kept the Spirit from using me as He wanted to? I felt my Father's presence enveloping me...loving me...coaxing me...urging me to a decision.

"Oh Father," I prayed, my face turned toward the city. *"Am I reading you right? Is this one more thing in my life that has to be changed before You can really use me? I'm not worthy of this incredible call to help the body, but if seeking the help of others makes it possible, you've got it. I YIELD RIGHT NOW!"*

The moment I made that surrender, excitement welled up inside me, almost bubbling over. What I was feeling was the pleasure of the Lord. My Father was happy with the decision and letting me know it. A word skyrocketed into my mind and exploded—*MARANATHA!* I recognized it as Paul's exclamation at the end of First Corinthians. It means...*"O, Lord come!"*

For a moment I was puzzled why the Holy Spirit would inflame that word in my mind—yet almost immediately I knew. The Lord's coming was near. If indeed I was His man to help His people get ready for His coming, that made me...A MARANATHA MAN! My heart pounded at the thought.

The words...MARANATHA MAN...glowed in my imagination like a neon sign. I knew what it was, God's *seal* that the job would be done! All He needed was that decision. Why did it take me so long to see it?

Jack's timing was perfect. I had heard what my Father wanted me to hear. I knew the fire I was feeling showed on the outside. As Jack drove home, I pondered the glorious vision of what could be done. The mounting excitement was so great, it was hard to contain. My feelings poured forth and spilled over on Jack. He couldn't keep his mind on his driving.

"You know what," he remarked, reflecting my enthusiasm, *"we may get another surprise when you share this with the rest of the board. Very likely the Lord has gone ahead of us and they'll be ready for this decision."*

That made it impossible to contain my excitement. *"Wow, if that's the case, Jack, we're on our way! With the final roadblock removed, what God has done in the past will be nothing compared to what He's going to do now with the help of the brethren! In fact, I don't see ANY limit!"*

CHAPTER FOURTEEN

A range of mountains separates the Los Angeles basin from the vast Mojave desert. Along the crest of this range is a road known as the Angeles Crest Highway. On Saturday afternoons, Margie and I often take a drive along this route. After a hard week's work, some time out of doors and away from the phone, makes for a refreshing change.

It was the Saturday following our board meeting. I felt the need to get away and ponder all that had happened. Margie packed a picnic lunch and we started out for an observation point, one of our favorite spots along this highway.

The rumble of the road, the purr of the engine and the comfort of a precious wife nestled against my side, provided just the right atmosphere for reflecting on the events of the past week.

Indeed it had been mind-boggling. After the visit with the evangelist, God led me to change the entire approach of the ministry. Then, the PC board, viewing the idea as an answer to our prayer, unanimously adopted the Maranatha Man concept. This was a bold move for us. In effect, it flung open the door of Personal Christianity to all who wanted to help in preparing for Christ's appearing.

I've always found it easy to discuss things with Margie. I wanted to review the Maranatha Man concept with her. If she understood it clearly, then I knew others would too. *"What does the word, 'Maranatha' mean to you, honey?"* I asked, ready to listen while she spoke from her heart.

Margie appreciates a chance to express her feelings. *"I know it means, 'O, Lord come.' And I like that because it is consistent with our call...'preparing for His appearing.' Maybe that's why the Holy Spirit told you you were His Maranatha Man. We've known for years He wanted you to help the Lord's people get ready for His coming. Now He's sealed our call with this word."*

"But you know dear," I interrupted gently, *"I'm not the ONLY Maranatha Man. ANYONE who loves the Lord's appearing and wants to help us get Christians ready, is a Maranatha Man. With time as short as it is, it's going to take a lot of Maranatha Men...and Women too!"*

"Women too!" she exclaimed. *"The ladies will like that. For once we'll be included as full partners and that's only right, since we're joint-heirs with Christ too."* It was like Margie to add the woman's touch.

She reached into the glove compartment for a small New Testament. Fanning the pages until her finger came to rest on a verse, she announced gleefully, *"Here it is! The apostle Paul says a CROWN OF RIGHTEOUSNESS is laid up for all who love the Lord's appearing. Why, there must be countless Christians who long for His return and would like to work with us to win that crown!"*

I was surprised and pleased to see how quickly she was laying hold of the concept. With one more piece of information, she'd have the whole picture. *"Turn to Revelation 19:7,"* I said, making a hurry-up gesture with my hand. I couldn't wait for her to get it all together and feel the magnitude of our ministry.

"I've found it," she purred. *"It's the place where John is speaking of the church as the bride of Christ, right?"*

"Right," I acknowledged. *"Loving the Lord's appearing, you see, is only part of the story. There's another feature just as important. The apostle John identifies it when he says...'THE MARRIAGE OF THE LAMB HAS COME AND HIS WIFE (BRIDE) HAS MADE HERSELF READY.*

"Margie, have you ever considered that the bride has to MAKE HERSELF ready? You don't hear much about that, do you? Yet—if she's not ready—CAN THE LORD COME?"

"Ahhhhhhhh...," she responded, *"now I see what*

224

you mean by MARANATHA MEN and WOMEN. Those who really love the Lord's appearing will do all they can to help His bride get ready, and in so doing, hasten His return! Oh Sam...are you thinking that all those who really care about His coming will want to help us get His bride ready!"

"I am. Isn't it beautiful!"

By then we had reached our parking spot. Getting out of the car, we climbed a short distance to the top of a giant boulder. From there the view was awe-inspiring. To the north was the desert. Marked in green and brown square sections, it resembled a giant checkerboard from afar. To the south lay the sprawling metropolis of Los Angeles stretching towards the Pacific Ocean. Just off shore, Catalina Island was in view.

While Margie unpacked the picnic basket, I perched myself on the boulder facing the desert. A warm breeze drifted up from the desert floor. A solitary eagle tested his acrobatic skills against a backdrop of fleecy, white clouds. My eyes hypnotically followed his soaring movements.

For a moment I forgot where I was. My thoughts raced backwards 45 years to another mountain—that one in Arizona. In my reverie, I could see myself leaning against that rusty ore car, staring off into endless space. There was a bird there, too, riding the air currents on outstretched wings.

Then came those thunderous questions for which I had had no answers, *"Who am I? Why am I here?"* I recalled the haunting feeling of being engulfed by life, yet not knowing why I existed.

A ground squirrel scampering in front of me interrupted my thoughts. I plucked a foxtail growing out of a crack in the boulder and twirled it between my hands. Forty-five years ago I didn't know who I was or why I was here.

But then, feelings of joy overwhelmed my spirit as I whispered to myself..."*I do now. You've come a long way, Sam.*"

Yet even as those thoughts surfaced, the Holy Spirit moved on my spirit. "*Yes,*" He breathed, "*you've come a long way. You know who you are and why you're here. You sit on that rock a very different man from the one I saw on that mountain in Arizona. But it has taken My sovereign work to get you to THIS mountain.*"

The sovereign work of God! I loved the very thought of it. Indeed He had done a lot of work in my life. Now He was reminding me of it. One by one He caused the steps of His plan to unfold before my imagination:

—being raised without a father, so He would be the only REAL FATHER I'd ever know;

—abandoning my fortune, so that serving Him would be more important than owning wealth;

—separating me from my brother, so that I would learn to put Him before any family member;

—humbling me before my seminary classmates, so that I didn't always have to be right;

226

—exposing me to the powerful example of Charles E. Fuller, so that I could handle criticism;

—showing me the appearance of C. S. Lovett's name on a book didn't make me a big shot;

—using a fire to convince me Personal Christianity was His and not mine;

—arranging for the evangelist to blast open the door of my stubborn heart to let others share in the joy and rewards of this ministry.

Yes, God had me where He wanted me. All of my life—through times, both good and bad—He had been patiently working to fashion a useable tool out of C.S. Lovett. Now I knew why He had perched me on this mountain top. I thought I had stopped at the observation point to see the sights below. But God had another view He wanted me to see—*the one behind*. He didn't want me to forget from whence I had come—from nothing. I was totally humbled.

"Lord Jesus...I love you," I whispered. My heart was flushed with love and joy. At the same time it was broken—realizing He had taken a worthless nothing and molded him into a useful servant.

My soul was singing "Amazing Grace" when Margie announced lunch was ready. In my spirit, I was already full. But I ate anyway. Looking at the lovely wife God had given me, I realized the vital role she had played in the softening of C. S. Lovett. I wanted to hold her and tell her what a precious gift she was. No one ever gets anywhere by himself.

Margie could always sense when something was going on between my Father and me. She began packing quietly, leaving me free to listen to Him.

I could feel His gentle nudging, His almost audible voice saying, *"Son, sit facing the city, I have more to say to you."*

I moved quickly to a spot looking out over the city of Los Angeles. In eager anticipation, my spirit answered back, *"Yes, Father?"*

"I've raised you up, Sam," said the still small voice within my spirit, *"to show My power in you. You are My Maranatha Man. I affirm that the job I've given you—preparing the body of Christ for My appearing—WILL BE DONE. But it will be accomplished through all the Maranatha Men and Women whom I will call."*

"If you call them, Father, what am I to do?"

"You do the thing for which I have now cleared the way. You INVITE them. My people will join with you in preparing for My appearing."

"Just invite? Is that all I'm to do?"

"Yes, son, that's all. I don't need any help in calling people. That's between Me and those whom I choose. Look at your life—I called you and you came. What I have done with you, I can do for any who obey My call. You invite them and I will call. If you do your part and trust Me to do Mine, you cannot fail. You will succeed and hasten My triumphant return."

"Thank you, Father, for this glorious job!"

228

I looked out on the sea of humanity making up southern California. How many Maranatha Men and Women did God have out there? How many would He raise up all over the world? I didn't know, but the prospect was infinite. That was God's business now—not mine. He said He would call them. I *knew* He would.

"Call them, Father," my spirit cried out. *"Maranatha!"*

INVITATION

Rarely do you come to the end of a book and find the author addressing you personally. But that's what I mean to do. The Holy Spirit has made it clear that I am to to INVITE YOU to become a MARANATHA MAN/WOMAN. He will CALL YOU. . .if it is His will for you to respond.

You've read the book. You know how God raised up this ministry to prepare His people for His appearing. Now here is my invitation:

I NEED YOU. I WANT YOUR HELP. SO I INVITE YOU TO GET IN TOUCH WITH ME AND WE'LL EXPLORE TOGETHER TO SEE IF IT IS HIS WILL FOR YOU TO PARTICIPATE AS A MARANATHA MAN/WOMAN.

Having read my invitation, you may wish to set the book aside and talk to the Lord, like this:

"Lord Jesus, do You want me to write to brother Lovett and find out if I should become a MARANATHA MAN or MARANATHA WOMAN? If so, may I have Your witness to my spirit? Amen."

If you feel kindly toward me and like the idea of praying for me, that will be the Holy Spirit's witness, you should write. When you do, I'll send you a free copy of "Be a Part of the MARANATHA VISION", a manual that shows specific ways you can get involved with me in fulfilling the vision. It is my way of making sure I am giving you the best possible invitation. Remember, the Lord said I was to invite. . .and He would call.

As you read this manual, you'll see why the MARANATHA VISION is not an impossible dream, but a heavenly calling. You'll love the idea of being a mara-natha man/woman, preparing yourself and others for the coming of the Lord. You'll find it rewarding, ful-filling. And you'll be laying up treasure in heaven be-yond your fondest dreams. In the process you and I will become personal friends. That's what makes it PERSONAL Christianity for me!

Joyously. . .in Jesus! *(Maranatha!)*

C.S. Lovett

SAMPLE LETTER

To make it easier for you to send for our free manual, "Be a Part of the MARANATHA VISION", I have prepared a sample letter you can use as a guide. As soon as you get your request in the mail, you'll feel the Lord's pleasure in your soul.

Dear Brother Lovett,   Date _____

I have read the story of your life and how God has brought you to the place where He can use you to help the body of Christ get ready for His appearing.

As I think about the Maranatha vision, my spirit warms to the idea of helping the bride of Christ make herself ready for His coming. I have accepted this as God's witness that I should write and let you know that I am a born-again Christian who loves the appearing of the Lord.

Would you please send me your free manual, "Be a Part of the MARANATHA VISION." I want to make sure I understand your invitation correctly. As I read, I will look to the Holy Spirit to show me what part He might want me to have in this exciting ministry.

Eagerly, in Christ,

Signed _____

If you do not wish to write a letter, simply use
the coupon below:

Dear Brother Lovett,

I have read the story of your life. As I think
about the Maranatha vision, my spirit warms to the
idea of helping the bride of Christ make herself
ready for His coming.

Would you please send me your free manual,
"Be a Part of the MARANATHA VISION." As I
read, I will look to the Holy Spirit to show me
what part He might want me to have in this
exciting ministry.

Name ——————————————————

Address ————————————————

City ———————————————————

State, Zip —————————————————

After filling in your name and address, enclose
this page in an envelope and mail to:

Dr. C. S. Lovett
Maranatha Vision
Personal Christianity
Box 549,
Baldwin Park, CA 91706